A HEIST BEFORE BEDTIME

A HEIST BEFORE BEDTIME

The Reverend Richard Coles

Illustrated by Eve O'Brien

wren & rook

First published in Great Britain in 2026 by Wren & Rook

Text copyright © Richard Coles 2026
Illustrations copyright © Eve O'Brien 2026
All rights reserved.

The right of Richard Coles and Eve O'Brien to be identified as the author and illustrator respectively of this Work has been asserted by them in accordance with the Copyright, Designs & Patents Act 1988.

ISBN: 978 1 5263 6766 2

10 9 8 7 6 5 4 3 2 1

Wren & Rook
An imprint of
Hachette Children's Group
Part of Hodder & Stoughton Limited
Carmelite House
50 Victoria Embankment
London EC4Y 0DZ

The authorised representative in the EEA is Hachette Ireland, 8 Castlecourt Centre, Dublin 15, D15 XTP3, Ireland (email: info@hbgi.ie)

An Hachette UK Company
www.hachette.co.uk
www.hachettechildrens.co.uk

Printed and bound in Great Britain by Clays Ltd, Elcograf S.p.A.

The website addresses (URLs) included in this book were valid at the time of going to press. However, it is possible that contents or addresses may have changed since the publication of this book. No responsibility for any such changes can be accepted by either the author or the publisher.

*For all the children who had
to endure my assemblies at
St Thomas' C of E Primary Boston,
The Knightsbridge School and
Finedon Mulso Junior School*

Contents

Preface	9
The Tall Tale of the Eiffel Tower	11
Has Anybody Seen My Brain?	29
The Lady Who Vanished	45
A Gruesome, Grisly Gunpowder Plot	61
The Maple Syrup Mystery	81
The Millennium Dome Diamond Heist	97
A Perfectly Preposterous Princess Prank	117
The Very Hungry Bear Break-in	137
The Fake Fairies of Cottingley	151
The Burglar and the Bugle	167
A Deadly Dangerous Bug Caper	185
The Million Dollar McDonald's Heist	201

Preface

Reader! Thanks for trying this book,
I'm glad you chose to take a look
At what some rascals nicked or took
Or conned their way to.
But I'm a vicar, so you see
It matters quite a lot to me
That, while you feel due empathy —
Don't do as they do.

A princess who once begged for bread
A conman who escaped a Fed,
A greedy bear asleep in bed
May blind us;
But rogues who failed to nick some bling
Some blokes who failed to kill a king
A thief who failed at everything
Remind us

That it's not cool to steal or cheat —
And if you do you'll feel the heat
And find your victories bittersweet
Eventually;
For soon enough you'll realise
That fooling folk and telling lies,
Like any dodgy enterprise,
Ends dreadfully.

The Tall Tale of the Eiffel Tower

Have you ever noticed how the world's **great** cities nearly always have an iconic building? So iconic that if you were to show a picture of it to anyone they will usually know where you mean. Big Ben? London. Taj Mahal? Agra. Burj Khalifa? Dubai.

I think the Eiffel Tower is the most iconic one of all. Nothing says Paris quite like it, and it is almost impossible to mix it up with being anywhere else. The Eiffel Tower is actually quite a recent arrival in Paris, unlike the Colosseum in Rome, which is nearly 2,000 years old, or the Great

Pyramid at Giza, which is TWICE as old again. The Eiffel Tower isn't even 150 years old. It first appeared over the Paris skyline in 1889, having been built for that year's World's Fair, a big global exhibition where lots of countries gather to celebrate industry and technology. Industry and technology went into the Eiffel Tower in **sack-loads!** It was the first iron structure of its kind in the world, built on a scale that would have been impossible before and made of more than 18,000 parts joined together with 2.5 million special iron fasteners called rivets.

As you can imagine, it was incredibly complicated to put together, and took two years to build, but the engineer who designed it, Gustave Eiffel, did such a good job that every part fitted together pretty much perfectly. And so an iron tower had been built, 300 metres tall and at that time by far the **tallest** building in the world! Paris returned the favour by naming it after him.

Nevertheless, when it opened there were plenty of critics who thought it looked like an alien craft had landed

THE TALL TALE OF THE EIFFEL TOWER

in the middle of their beloved city. 'Paris is Notre-Dame!' they said. 'Paris is the Arc de Triomphe!' But others really liked it, and after a while they started calling it the 'Iron Lady', which is a bit confusing for British people, because that's what we called Margaret Thatcher when she was Prime Minister in the 1980s (and although quite spiky, Mrs Thatcher looked nothing like the Eiffel Tower). Soon the great iron structure was a **wonder of the world**, perhaps the first truly iconic building – so iconic that when Hitler invaded France in 1940, he made a trip to Paris so he could be seen standing in front of it and everyone else could see that he was now in charge. Now, in happier times, the Eiffel Tower sells more tickets to visitors than any other structure in the world – about six million per year.

There was no doubt about it, the Eiffel Tower had become the symbol of not only Paris but all of France. So why on earth did *anyone* fall for it when in 1925 a man called Victor Lustig tried to sell it?

Yes, that's right. In 1925 Count Victor Lustig (he wasn't

a count, by the way; he made that up) contacted some carefully chosen scrap-metal dealers in France, telling them he had been authorised to sell the Eiffel Tower for scrap and would they like to offer him some cash in exchange for dismantling it and carrying off all that lovely iron. This was not quite as outlandish as it sounds, because the tower was originally intended only as a temporary structure, due to be dismantled in 1909. Therefore it had not been built to last and needed a lot of maintenance. It probably *would* have come down in 1909, had it not all of a sudden become very useful as a telecommunications tower. Anyway, every year the cost of looking after it mounted up and that's how dodgy Victor saw his opportunity. So exactly *how* did Victor carry out his plan . . . ?

First he booked a room at the very posh Hôtel de Crillon in Paris, somehow persuading the staff there to turn it into a temporary office for him. Then he found a forger to make some official-looking (but actually fake) stationery and wrote to the bosses of France's leading scrap-

THE TALL TALE OF THE EIFFEL TOWER

metal businesses pretending to be the Deputy Director-General of the Ministry of Posts and Telegraphs. His letter invited them all to a meeting to discuss a profitable business proposal. They all came, and Victor made his sales pitch. He explained to them that the cost of maintaining the tower was just too much for the city of Paris to bear so a decision had been made to scrap it. If any of them wanted to buy the tower for scrap they should make him an offer and he would award the contract to the best one.

Ten thousand tonnes of iron was a tempting prospect indeed, so perhaps that made the scrap-metal dealers a bit less curious than they should have been about this so-called Deputy Director-General of the Ministry of Posts and Telegraphs. Victor *then* said that scrapping the tower would be controversial – the Iron Lady was world famous after all – so the agreement had to be reached discreetly, which meant no one could know anything about it until the deal was done. This was very clever, but Victor was not just a conman, he was one of the most successful conmen there ever was. During his life he had forty-seven aliases (meaning he used forty-seven false names and identities), a suitcase full of disguises (including a rabbi and a priest) and he would even go on to con the world's most notorious gangster, someone who would murder his enemies just as easily as swatting flies.

So Victor had chutzpah (this is one of my favourite words; it means brass neck, boldness, Artful-Dodgeriness and other things like that). He could charm the birds out of the trees; he could talk the fish out of the seas – and especially a scrap-metal dealer called André Poisson (which, by the way, means Andy Fish). Andy Fish – sorry, I mean Monsieur Poisson – wasn't one of the biggest scrap dealers but he was very **ambitious**. So what better way to become bigger and better than by winning the contract to scrap the Eiffel Tower?

Like all successful conmen, Victor had done his homework. He had learned everything he could about the Eiffel Tower and its construction, so he sounded

THE TALL TALE OF THE EIFFEL TOWER

like he knew what he was talking about. He was good at psychology too; he took one careful look at Mr Fish – sorry, Monsieur Poisson – and instantly saw what he was looking for: ambition. Conmen love ambitious people because when we're really focused on getting what we want, we can become blind and deaf to the red lights and alarms that normally go off when we think someone might be trying to fool us. So Victor befriended the ambitious Monsieur Poisson, and even took him away for a weekend in Bordeaux before telling him his bid had been successful. The Eiffel Tower would be his for a bargain price of **1.2 million francs** (about a million quid in today's money).

There was just one *tiny* thing though. In order to close the deal, it would be necessary for Monsieur Poisson to quietly take care of Victor's expenses, which he had run up in the course of the negotiations. By 'expenses' he really meant a bribe. This would not have been seen as that unusual; Victor was not the only person – then or now – working for a government who would expect his 'expenses'

—— A HEIST BEFORE BEDTIME ——

to be paid. He suggested a sum of 70,000 francs (about £50,000 in today's money), which was quite some expenses claim, but Monsieur Poisson was by now completely committed to buying the Eiffel Tower, so he agreed. He paid the 70,000 francs of 'expenses' in cash and then he gave a further 1.2 million francs for the Eiffel Tower itself. After that he went home to celebrate the greatest deal of his career, while waiting for the paperwork to arrive.

But the paperwork did not arrive. Victor, on the other hand, arrived in Vienna with 70,000 of Monsieur Poisson's francs.

―――― THE TALL TALE OF THE EIFFEL TOWER ――――

Imagine what it was like for Monsieur Poisson to realise that the greatest deal of his career was a complete con? Instead of suddenly upgrading himself to France's greatest scrap-metal dealer he had allowed himself to be fooled, lost 70,000 francs and was left looking a right **Poisson d'Avril**. Do you know what that is? It's what April Fools are called in France.

Meanwhile Victor was living it up in Vienna, a city he knew well because he came from Austria-Hungary (as that part of the world was known back then). Vienna was its very grand capital city. And, as everyone would soon find out, 'Count Victor' was not a nobleman at all, just plain Victor Lustig, born into a prosperous family in a little town in Bohemia (an old country that used to be part of the Czech Republic) in 1890.

Victor had been **a super-bright child** who learned loads of languages and went on to study in Paris. He decided to launch his career as a con artist when he was just nineteen, working the transatlantic liners that cruised between Europe and the United States. He would travel first class – nothing but the best for Victor – and pretend to be a producer of Broadway shows, then persuade other passengers to invest in them. When they did, he would disappear with all their money.

Then when the First World War came along in 1914, Victor moved to the United States. He was eventually caught trying to con a bank in Missouri and sent back to France. That's when he returned to Paris and came up with the idea to sell the Eiffel Tower.

Anyway, back to *that* story – there he was now in Vienna, spending Monsieur Poisson's money and probably having a really good time eating really good cakes like Sachertorte (if you've never had one, it is a sponge sandwich with apricot jam in the middle covered with a perfectly smooth and glossy chocolate coat). If it were *me* in Vienna with 70,000 francs to spend I think I would have eaten a lot of cake, but a good conman never really takes time off and Victor had another idea. You see, he *did* imagine what it was like

THE TALL TALE OF THE EIFFEL TOWER

to be Monsieur Poisson, and he figured that Mr Poisson would be so embarrassed about having fallen for his story and handing over all that money that he wouldn't go to the police or even tell anybody about it. So if nobody knew Victor had sold the Eiffel Tower, then **why not try and sell it again?** And that is exactly what he did.

Victor went back to Paris and invited some more scrap-metal dealers – different ones this time – to a meeting at his office in another posh hotel, telling them the same story he had told Monsieur Poisson: the Eiffel Tower was to be sold for scrap. This time, however, Victor was not so lucky. One of the dealers became suspicious and notified the authorities. But when the police came for Victor he managed to give them the slip and off he went back to the United States.

There, he continued his fascinating career of swindling people. His boldest con was undoubtedly cheating one of **the world's most famous gangsters**, Al Capone, out of $5,000. Al Capone, aka Scarface, was the most notorious gangster in Chicago and the boss responsible for the St Valentine's Day Massacre, when seven members of a rival gang were murdered in broad daylight by his men. After that, Capone's enemies then tried to have *him* assassinated, but the hitmen they sent – a dozen or so – were all murdered before they got anywhere near him.

So as you can see, you *didn't* mess with Scarface. Well, you didn't unless you were Victor Lustig. One of the ways gangsters make their living is by lending people money. These loans are not like ones from the bank; they are private arrangements for people who either wouldn't want a bank to know what they needed the money for, or who were so desperate for money that no bank would lend them a cent. In return, the gangsters demanded very high fees – so high that a lot of the time it was impossible to repay them. Why would a gangster lend someone money if they couldn't repay it? Because the gangster would then pretty much own the person who owed them the dosh, that's why. That meant they could get them to do whatever

THE TALL TALE OF THE EIFFEL TOWER

they wanted – or else. Obviously most people would do anything they could to stay away from gangsters, but not Victor. He borrowed $50,000 from Scarface. Then instead of paying him back in expensive instalments (Scarface would have made him pay back MUCH more than $50,000 for the 'favour' of having loaned him the money) he went straight back to him and said someone had robbed him and the $50,000 was all gone. Well, how do you think *that* went down? But then Victor produced the $50,000 after all (which he said he had somehow managed to raise), offering it to Scarface as a gesture of respect. Victor also promised that any extra charges would be paid in full. Al Capone was so impressed by **Victor's bravery** (because I don't think anyone else would have had the nerve to try something like that) that he not only let him off the extra payments, he actually gave him a *reward* of $5,000. Not a bad day's work . . . $5,000 for doing pretty much nothing. And to have conned Scarface himself was a feat without equal.

A HEIST BEFORE BEDTIME

But my favourite of all his cons – after selling the Eiffel Tower twice, that is – was the Rumanian Box. Again, this sounds so daft it's hard to imagine anyone falling for it but, believe me, they did. It worked like this: Victor would befriend someone and tell them he had a special box that could make **fake banknotes** so perfectly they would never be detected. He would then arrange to meet them at his hotel, where he would show them this mysterious box, made from wood and about the size of a trunk, with dials and levers and two slots. He would then take a hundred-dollar bill, insert it into one of the slots, pull the lever and say it would take six hours for the process to be completed so off they should go to have a nice lunch or a stroll somewhere while they waited.

When they returned, Victor would pull another lever and an identical hundred-dollar bill popped out along with the original one. Of course, it was not an identical hundred-dollar bill at all. Victor had taken a load of real hundred-dollar bills out of the bank, all numbered

THE TALL TALE OF THE EIFFEL TOWER

in sequence. He'd then taken two of those bills, carefully changed the last number on the second one to match the number on the first so it looked identical, and secretly put that one in the box with the original. When they both popped out, Victor's victims fell for his trick and thought the box really had **magically** duplicated real-looking money. After that, Victor took his victims to the bank and handed over the original unaltered hundred-dollar bill to have it authenticated. Then off they both went for a drink to celebrate, during which Victor would casually mention that he *might* just be tempted to part with the Rumanian Box if someone made him the right offer. 'Me, me, me!' the victim said, so Victor would sell it to them for thousands of dollars. Upon which they would take it home, insert a hundred-dollar bill, turn the lever and come back the next day to find . . . just the same hundred-dollar bill that they had put into the box, while Victor was nowhere to be found.

Here is a good tip for life: if anyone offers you free

money, **do not believe them** – THERE IS NO SUCH THING! But people do fall for it now and then, because the thought of free money is so tempting.

So what eventually happened to the one and only Victor Lustig? 'Oh, what a tangled web we weave when first we practise to deceive', the saying goes, and so it was with Victor Lustig. In spite of a long and successful career as a conman, he was eventually caught out trying to con a woman with whom he was romantically involved. She discovered that she was not the only one, so she reported him to the police and he was finally arrested in New York in 1935. Sure enough, the police found loads of counterfeit (fake) dollar bills in a locker Victor kept at a subway station, and so he was sent to jail to await trial. **But Victor wasn't going to go down that easily!** The day before the trial, Victor made a rope by knotting together sheets he had helped himself to from the laundry cart. He then knocked out a window and lowered himself from his cell in broad daylight, pretending to be the window

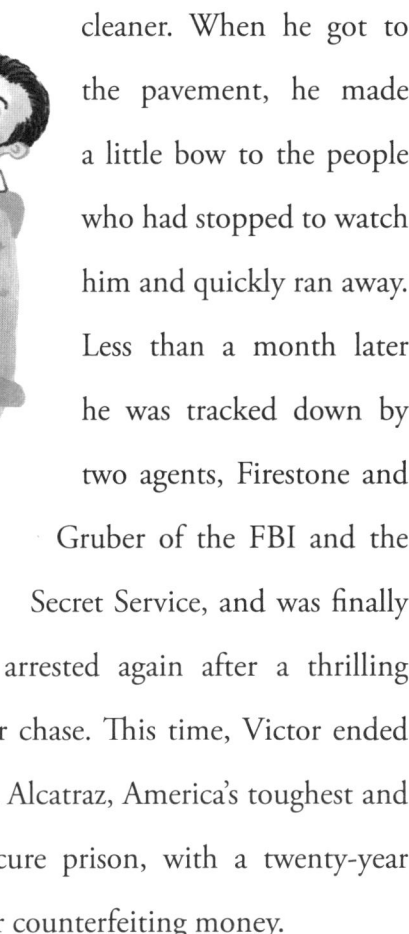

cleaner. When he got to the pavement, he made a little bow to the people who had stopped to watch him and quickly ran away. Less than a month later he was tracked down by two agents, Firestone and Gruber of the FBI and the Secret Service, and was finally arrested again after a thrilling car chase. This time, Victor ended up in Alcatraz, America's toughest and most secure prison, with a twenty-year sentence for counterfeiting money.

How would Victor get out of this one? He tried his best to play the system, putting in more than a thousand requests to be moved from the super-tough prison to a medical centre on the grounds of poor health, but those lies, nowhere near his worst, would be the undoing of Victor Lustig. For one day he told the prison guards – again – he was feeling very unwell and needed treatment, but the guards, so fed up with his fake requests for a medical transfer, ignored him instead. But this time Victor really was unwell, with pneumonia, and by the time he was transferred to a medical centre it was too late, and there Victor Lustig died, aged only fifty-seven.

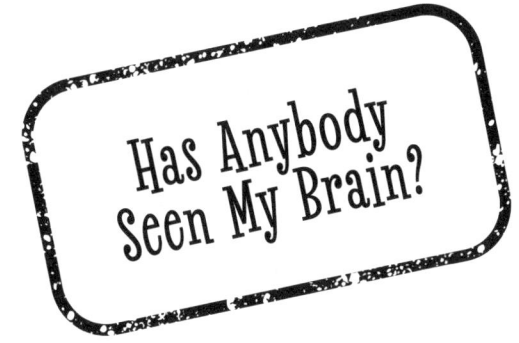

Has Anybody Seen My Brain?

Who is the brainiest person that ever lived? That's a hard question to answer, because people are brainy in different ways. Some would say Elon Musk – not only an engineering genius and space pioneer, but **the richest man in the world**. That sounds pretty brainy, doesn't it? Others might say Leonardo da Vinci, who painted the *Mona Lisa* (there is a story about her later in this book). Leonardo was also a poet, a scientist and an inventor, which all sounds VERY brainy! Or how about Marie Curie, who won two Nobel Prizes for nuclear physics and pioneered new treatments for cancer? Or maybe there is someone we've never even heard of who did their clever thing while cleverly managing to remain entirely unknown? That would be *really* brainy. But if you want an example of a **super-brainy** person who loads of people would recognise and very few would argue with, I suggest Albert Einstein.

Albert Einstein was the most famous scientist of his day when he died in 1955 in the United States, where he had gone to live after Hitler came to power in his own country, Germany. Some might say he looked like a famous scientist too, with shaggy white hair, a lively and curious manner, thick specs and a big moustache. Some also say he was the greatest physicist who ever lived, greater even than Isaac Newton, who discovered gravity. Gravity was – and is – already everywhere actually, but in 1687 in Lincolnshire an apple fell on Newton's head, which gave him the idea that a force you cannot see attracted the apple towards the ground, or so the story goes. But back to Einstein . . .

Einstein was born in Germany in 1879. At first, no

one thought he was brainy at all; his parents even worried that he wasn't developing properly when he was a little boy because he seemed so slow to understand anything. Well, he ended up with a Nobel Prize; a mountain and a chemical were both named after him; and he was named 'Person of the Century' by *Time* magazine. So don't be too quick to write anyone off, OK?

Einstein pulled off his most amazingly brainy achievement while he was working in the Patent Office in Switzerland, which sounds like a fairly ordinary job for a world-class brainbox. But it was there, in 1905, that he came up with his theory that would change the world. It is called the Theory of General Relativity, and you often see it written as **$E = mc^2$**, which looks like the name of a rapper to me. But it isn't that at all – it's a simple maths formula. Simple, perhaps, but it took a brain the size of Switzerland to figure it out. OK, OK, it wasn't *really* the size of Switzerland, as you'll find out shortly.

Anyway, the theory meant that the young (ish) Albert

A HEIST BEFORE BEDTIME

Einstein realised that space and time were connected in a way no one had realised before. It was such a novel idea that at first very few people understood it (few people understand it today, including me, so if you want to know more, find a friendly physics expert to ask). This meant Einstein had a job to prove it even to the people who *did*

understand it. In fact, he had to wait fourteen years before he finally could, when on 29 May 1919 there was an eclipse of the sun. Einstein declared that astronomers observing it would see that light did exactly what he'd predicted it would do back in 1905. And it did. What did it do exactly? I'm about to tell you: **it got bent by gravity!**

If Einstein was right about *that*, then his whole theory was right. Soon there were headlines in newspapers all over the world saying we were going to have to rethink maths and physics and everything to do with maths and physics (which is just about *everything*). **Einstein was hailed as a genius.**

That, I feel sure you will agree, is SERIOUSLY brainy. And *that* is why Einstein must have had a brain the size of Switzerland! But then how did he manage to fit it inside his head? Well, let's see, shall we . . .

When Einstein died in 1955, his last spoken words were in German, and the nurse who was looking after him did not understand that language. So, rather annoyingly, those words of wisdom are lost forever. But what we did *not* lose is his incredible brain. This is what happened next.

After Einstein's death, the doctor on duty at the hospital examined his body to find out *how* he had died. It had been Einstein's wish to be cremated, but this particular doctor thought it would be a shame if such a magnificent brain was reduced to ashes along with the rest of his body. *Wouldn't it be better if it could be studied, to see if there is anything unusual about it?* he thought. *And if there is, then we might be able to understand the brain better and that would be such a good thing that surely Einstein could not possibly object?* Well, the doctor was *so* sure of this that he removed Einstein's brain without telling anyone. He didn't even ask Einstein's family for their permission.

Instead he took a special saw, cut off the top of Einstein's head and carefully **removed the brain** (complete with his eyes, which were still attached), and put it in a special preserving chemical. After that he handed the rest of the body over to the undertakers (the people who prepare dead bodies for burial or cremation). The very next day, what was left of Einstein was cremated, with just his family in attendance.

Meanwhile the doctor, who was called Thomas Harvey, took the brain to his lab at the University of Pennsylvania. There he weighed it and found it to be 1,230 grams, which is about the same weight as a chihuahua and an average size for a human brain. Then Dr Harvey photographed the brain (it looked a bit like a giant walnut) and even had it painted by an artist who had done some nice portraits of his children. He then cut it up into 240 little cubes, sliced *them* up incredibly finely and put the slices on microscopic slides stained with chemicals. Through the lens of a microscope, he could now see the tiniest structures (called cells) that made up Einstein's brain. Dr Harvey made twelve sets of these slides. He kept two for himself and sent the other ten sets to doctors all over the world – doctors he thought best qualified to examine them. He also removed the eyes and gave them to Einstein's eye doctor.

Meanwhile, a man called Otto Nathan was helping Einstein's family to take care of his affairs after his death and when he heard about all this, **he was furious**. He summoned Dr Harvey to his apartment and demanded to know what he was doing with Einstein's brain. Luckily, Dr Harvey managed to persuade him that it was a proper scientific inquiry, and that it was a bit unclear, but when Einstein was alive he *had* consented to have some tests done on his brain. His son, Hans Einstein, knew about this so eventually in the interest of science he gave his blessing to Dr Harvey – he *could* examine his father's brain on the condition that the results were published only in proper scientific journals.

But what sort of results? Dr Harvey was interested to see if the cells in Einstein's brain were different from other people's brain cells, so he spent ages looking at them through his microscope. Of course, by now he wasn't the only one; all the other scientists he had sent samples to would be conducting their own research too.

Except, funnily enough, it seems they didn't. If *I* were a brain specialist and someone sent *me* the most famous brain in the entire world to study, **I'd drop everything and crack on with it**. But that isn't what happened. Quite a few people didn't even bother to reply when the slides arrived, and those who *did* simply said there didn't seem to be anything unusual about the brain samples at all. Why would there be? Why should the brain of someone who thought super-brainy thoughts look different from someone who just thought ordinary thoughts? Surely it's the thought that's different, rather than the brain? Others didn't agree, including the US Army, who were very interested in the brain. At that time the military was just beginning to get interested in how super intelligence could be used to get ahead of the enemy. America's main enemy at that time, the Soviet Union, was also examining the brains of its brightest scientists and thinkers after they died.

Either way, the scientific report promised by Dr Harvey about the greatest brain of the day did not appear and the story eventually faded away from the news. Twenty years and a bit went by and in 1978 a journalist at the *New Jersey Monthly* called Steven Levy was thinking about running a story on Einstein; after all, it was almost the 100th anniversary of Einstein's birth. But what should they write about? That's how Steven Levy was given an unusual assignment: **'Find Einstein's brain!'**

So off Steven went on a brain hunt. It had been such a long time since anyone had thought about Einstein's brain that at first he couldn't find any clues about where it might be (remember, this was before the Internet). Steven contacted the hospital at Princeton where Einstein had died and where Dr Harvey had worked, but there were no leads there. Next he tracked down Otto Nathan, the man who looked after the Einstein family's affairs. Otto confirmed the brain had been removed by Dr Harvey but that he had no idea where the doctor was now. If Steven had Google he would probably have tracked down the brain in half a second, but it was twenty years before Google was invented. So instead, Steven contacted the American Medical Association, found Dr Harvey's middle initial – which was S for Stoltz – and *finally* got an address for him in Kansas, USA.

Next, he called the telephone company and asked if they had a number for a Dr Harvey in that city: they did. Steven dialled the number and when the doctor answered, he explained the reason for the call. 'I'm trying to find a brain. Einstein's brain. You don't happen to know anything about it?' Steven asked – or something like that anyway. To which Dr Harvey replied, 'No way!' or something like *that*, but the journalist was persistent and eventually Dr Harvey agreed to meet him.

And that's how Steven Levy got on a plane to Kansas, where he would meet Dr Harvey in his lab in Wichita. They talked for a bit, during which Dr Harvey was reluctant to give anything away, but Steven kept asking and asking . . . and asking. In the end he said he'd flown thousands of miles so did Dr Harvey at least have a photograph of the brain he could see to make the trip **worth his trouble?** Dr Harvey hesitated and then said, 'I do have a bit of the gross here.'

The *gross*?

That's right – *the gross material.* At first Steven didn't understand what this meant but then he realised Dr Harvey was talking about the *actual* brain. Sure enough, Dr Harvey walked over to a cardboard box marked 'CIDER' and took out what looked like a glass cookie jar. But it did not contain cookies. Instead, inside the jar was DICED BRAIN! And not just any brain – **Einstein's brain!** Arguably the cleverest brain **in the entire world**. It wasn't locked away in a bank vault, or protected by security guards, it was just sitting in a box marked 'CIDER' waiting for this very moment to be rediscovered. MISSION ACCOMPLISHED! Steven had found Einstein's brain, or some good chunks of it anyway. And what about the research that Dr Harvey had promised back in 1955, when he had posted slices of Einstein's brain out to all those other scientists? 'It's coming,' said Dr Harvey. 'In about a year.'

But that never came. So the brain was returned to Einstein's family, and *they* arranged for it to be sent to experts to study. A few chunks of it were put in an old mayonnaise jar and sent to a neuroanatomist at the University of California. Some other chunks were sent to some other neuroscientists. This is what they discovered.

Einstein's brain, a bit ropey now after all those years, was indeed a bit **different to other brains**. It was actually a bit smaller than average but it contained an unusually large number of cells called glia, which are sort of cells that look after the main cells, but just as important. Furthermore, the Sylvian fissure, which is a kind of cleft dividing the left hand and the right hand sides of the brain, was missing. The brain also had four ridges on the front, whereas most people have three. And finally, the part of the brain that works out vision and space was noticeably **bigger** than most other people's. Einstein had sometimes said he tended to think in pictures rather than in words, so perhaps Dr Harvey's hunch was right after all – that the unique braininess of Einstein was indeed down to its shape and content.

You might be wondering what happened to Einstein's brain in the end. Well, half of it is now in the Mütter Medical Museum in Philadelphia, not far from the lab where Dr Harvey first cut it up. When Dr Harvey died his family donated what he had left of the brain to the National Museum of Health and Medicine near Washington DC. And there it sits to this day, preserved alongside bits of

President Abraham Lincoln following his assassination (and bits of his assassin too), President Ulysses S. Grant's tumour (which is a mass of cancerous cells) and the skeleton of Abe, who was the very first monkey to travel into space.

The Lady Who Vanished

If you ever visit Paris, top of the list of places to go is the Louvre, one of the world's greatest museums. It's worth going early to beat the crowds, but no matter how early you get there you'll still have to queue to see its most famous exhibit, the *Mona Lisa* – the portrait of the young noblewoman called Lisa del Giocondo sitting with folded hands and a half-smile in front of a rocky landscape of a winding river. The painting was commissioned by her husband from the dazzling artist Leonardo da Vinci at the beginning of the 1500s in Florence, Italy. It was

A HEIST BEFORE BEDTIME

immediately hailed as a **masterpiece**, and has been by every generation since. Today the *Mona Lisa* is the most famous painting in the world, and since 1797 she has sat in the Louvre, looking out of her frame (now behind bulletproof glass) at the numberless visitors gazing back at her. The image has been reproduced on a million fridge magnets, a million tea towels and has been borrowed by everyone from *The Simpsons*, to the Minions at the opening ceremony for the 2024 Olympics in Paris.

But how did the *Mona Lisa* go from famous to mega-famous? To understand that we need to go back in time to 1911, when she encountered a man called Vincenzo Peruggia, who pulled off the **most famous art heist ever** when he somehow managed to steal Leonardo's masterpiece right from under the noses of hundreds of guards.

Vincenzo was born in 1881 and grew up in the Italian Alps – perhaps the rocky background in the painting he pinched reminded him of his childhood? He moved to

Paris in 1908 with the dream of becoming a painter. But that didn't work out so he eventually found a job as a technician instead, helping protect works of art by framing and glazing (putting glass in their frames), and moving them around. He must have been good at it because he got to work at the Louvre with its magnificent collection of paintings. Many of the treasures there came from Napoleon, France's great emperor, who a century earlier had rampaged through Europe conquering nations and helping himself to their treasures as he went. The richest pickings were to be had in Italy, and perhaps the most famous Italian artist was Leonardo da Vinci, who was not only a painter but a scientist, an engineer, an architect and a musician too. He is most celebrated as a painter though, with not one but two of the world's most famous paintings to his name. As well as the *Mona Lisa*, da Vinci painted *The Last Supper*, which shows Jesus and the disciples dining on the night before his arrest.

Anyway, back to Vincenzo Peruggia. By the time

Vincenzo grew up, Italy was an independent nation after years of being ruled by other countries. He was fiercely patriotic and extremely proud that his homeland had produced so many wonders in art, literature, architecture, sculpture and food (don't forget the food!). It must have been challenging for him to work every day in a building full of many treasures that were only there because a foreign conqueror like Napoleon had looted them.

So one day Vincenzo decided to do something about it. It is not absolutely clear whether he just decided to do this something there and then or if it had been carefully planned. But we do know that he turned up at the Louvre, borrowed a white coat to make it look like he was working there that day and hid in a caretaker's cupboard. When the visitors had dwindled away and the footsteps of the 200 guards receded as they did their final inspection, Vincenzo made his move. He found his way to the Salon Carré where they kept the *Mona Lisa*, carefully removed its glass case and hid it, took the painting down from its mount and removed it from the frame. Then he covered it with a sheet and made his way down a service staircase to a door that led to the street. His heart must have been racing for he was about to make off with one of France's greatest treasures from its greatest museum. But then his heart must have almost *stopped*, because when he turned the handle of the door he discovered it was **locked**. What was he going to do? He found a screwdriver and tried to unscrew the doorknob, but before he could, he heard the sounds of footsteps approaching.

He must have cursed his luck, having come so far only to be caught mere metres from the street. But luck turned out to be kind to him. The footsteps came from a plumber called Monsieur Sauvet. He didn't for a moment think there was anything suspicious about Vincenzo (even though he had the museum's most famous painting tucked under his arm). It wasn't unheard of for workers at the Louvre to get stuck behind locked doors. So Monsieur Sauvet wished Vincenzo a good morning and then used his key to open the door. And that is how Vincenzo and the *Mona Lisa* simply **walked out into the street**.

Imagine how it must have felt to cross the Rue de Rivoli with Leonardo's masterpiece under your arm! I wonder if he hurried, for surely the disappearance of the mysterious smiling woman would be noticed as soon as the staff arrived? How far would he get before the alarm was raised?

The answer is: all the way home! One of the more surprising twists in this story is how long it took for anyone to even notice this priceless painting was missing. It wasn't unusual for paintings to be removed from time to time to be cleaned and repaired, or loaned to other museums and galleries, so an empty space on the wall would not have necessarily aroused suspicion.

The next day a painter called Louis Béroud arrived to make a sketch of the *Mona Lisa*. Instead of Leonardo's masterpiece hanging on the wall, there was simply a gap and four iron pegs. So Béroud asked one of the guards where she had gone. At first the guard thought the painting had been taken off somewhere to be photographed, but when Béroud checked with the man in charge of the Salon

Carré they discovered that no such thing had happened. The *Mona Lisa* was in fact simply . . . **GONE**.

Panic followed. How could someone have got in and out of the locked Louvre and taken its most prized exhibit from under the noses of 200 guards? The museum was put into immediate lockdown and sixty police officers were dispatched to the gallery.

'We know who came in and out,' said the senior detective. 'This investigation will only take two to three days.' Everyone involved was so keen to catch the thief that a ship leaving for New York was stopped at the harbour and searched, but there was no painting. Then another ship arriving in New York from France was searched – but no *Mona Lisa* was found on board that either. Meanwhile, at the Louvre all the permanent staff were interviewed but still nothing turned up, so the investigators turned to temporary staff and contractors. And it wasn't long before Vincenzo was summoned to the police station to make a statement. But *he* didn't turn up so officers went to his flat and knocked on his door. Vincenzo let them in and invited them to sit at the kitchen table to take his statement. What they didn't know as they listened to Vincenzo and made notes was that he had hidden the *Mona Lisa* under the very table they were sitting at. She was right there, smiling up at them, **and they missed her!** I don't think they can have been very good detectives because the judge in charge of the investigation had instructed them to look out especially for glaziers – exactly Vincenzo's job – for who would know better how to remove a glass case from a painting than the person who put it there?

That's right – not only did Vincenzo remove the glass to steal the painting, he had also made it. And when he hid it, he left a whacking great thumbprint on it! But nobody bothered to take his fingerprints so a match could not be made. Well, it could have been, actually, because following a previous investigation the police already had Vincenzo's fingerprints on file. However, nobody checked, so he never made it on to the list of official suspects. Days turned into weeks and the police were still no nearer to solving the mystery.

The newspapers turned on the government and the museum authorities for failing to rescue the *Mona Lisa* and arrest her abductor. To be fair, the museum had done a pretty useless job of protecting her. When the director, who was away at the time of the theft, was notified, he replied that stealing the painting would be about as likely as stealing the towers of Notre-Dame Cathedral and that there must have been some kind of mistake. The arts minister had been so confident no one could break into the Louvre that when he went on holiday he joked he should only be contacted by the office in the unimaginable event of the *Mona Lisa* being stolen. Imagine how he felt when he actually *got* that call?

The theft may have been a loss to the Louvre but it was a gift to newspapers all around Europe and the world, who wrote lots of stories about the investigation. One paper even reported the French police had called on the great thief Arsène Lupin for assistance. Lupin was as famous in France as Sherlock Holmes was in England but, like Holmes, Lupin is a fictional character and not a real person, so not much good to the investigation at all. The story was so widely reported, and there were so many offers of a reward for the painting's recovery, that it was said to have been sighted everywhere from New York to Berlin, and the investigation was overwhelmed with calls from people who thought they knew where it was. Only they didn't. When the Louvre reopened to the public so many people were fascinated by the story they queued for hours just to look at the gap where the painting had once hung.

Two whole years went by and still no painting. The government looked hopelessly incompetent; the head of the Louvre was replaced; the investigators tore their hair out in frustration; but there was still no sign of the *Mona Lisa*. Theories about her disappearance became wilder and wilder. There was even one that briefly blamed the famous painter Pablo Picasso.

A HEIST BEFORE BEDTIME

Where *was* that elusive painting? Well, I can tell you where she was. On her way home to Italy with Vincenzo, who hid her in a trunk and took the train to Florence, where Leonardo had started to paint her more than four centuries earlier.

The final twist in the plot came when a couple of years after the theft Vincenzo wrote to some relatives telling them that he was about to come into some money, enough money to change all of their lives. This meant Vincenzo was going to try to sell the *Mona Lisa*. But how? She now had one of the most recognisable faces in the entire world and the heist was a huge international story. Who on earth would want to buy a painting like that? Imagine having to explain her presence on your wall to a visitor. '*Mona Lisa*? Oh yes, a bit like her, I suppose, but the hair's quite different . . . Anyway, fancy a smoothie?'

Though there is another way of making money from stealing art. If there's a reward for recovering it, you could always claim *that*. And when people asked where you had got the painting from you could just say, 'Oh, I found it in a bus shelter,' or, **'Can you believe it was simply left on the street?'**

It is not clear what Vincenzo had in mind, but he wrote to the owner of an art gallery in Florence, signing his name Leonardo V and saying he had the painting and was prepared to hand it over for 500,000 lire (about £2m in today's money). And so a meeting was arranged with the director of one of Florence's most famous museums, the Uffizi, to see if it really was the *Mona Lisa*. But the meeting did not go as planned for Vincenzo. The police were informed; they arrived at the hotel where Vincenzo was staying, promptly arrested him and found the painting, missing for two years, hidden under his bed.

The *Mona Lisa* had been discovered; the thief had been apprehended. And the hotel was swiftly renamed La Gioconda in honour of its temporary resident.

And so Vincenzo was sent to jail to await trial, and the *Mona Lisa* was temporarily displayed at the Uffizi, where crowds of 30,000 people came to see her. So many people visited that the police had to be called to keep order. She then went on a short tour of Italy before being dispatched back to Paris where she was ceremoniously reinstalled in the Louvre on 4 January 1914. **It was front-page news all over the world.**

Meanwhile, back in Florence the front-page news was Vincenzo, hailed as a hero for returning one of Italy's greatest treasures to the city where she had been created. Of course, theft is theft, and when he appeared before the judge, Vincenzo *was* found guilty. But he was also given the lightest of sentences – serving only seven months before he was released. Vincenzo subsequently served in the Italian army during the First World War and was held captive again – this time as a prisoner of war until peace came in 1918. And after that, Vincenzo married, had a daughter and returned to Paris, where he worked as a painter and decorator. He died on his forty-fourth birthday in 1925.

Meanwhile, the *Mona Lisa* had become **the most**

famous painting in the entire world. All those weeks in the news had turned her into one of the most recognisable faces of the age, and since then her fame has grown and grown. She had some more adventures along the way, spirited away by the French government in the Second World War and hidden for a while when Hitler and his armies took Paris. She has been attacked with a knife, with paint and even with cake, and **she survived them all**, even if she is now protected by bulletproof glass. Her insurance value has been estimated at a billion dollars and she is such a draw that you are only allowed to look at her for a few moments when you visit the Louvre, so that other people can have their turn.

And what about Vincenzo? After all that, *was* he a hero who restored to Italy the painting Napoleon had looted all those years ago?

The answer is no. The *Mona Lisa*, in spite of what Vincenzo thought, was not brought to France by the warrior Napoleon, but by Leonardo himself. When

A HEIST BEFORE BEDTIME

he came to France in 1516 to live out his final years, he brought with him the *Mona Lisa* for company, a painting that he never thought finished, and that he hung on to until his dying day. And France has hung on to her ever since, not as the loot of a conquering general but as a work of genius that belongs not to Italy, not to France, but to the whole world.

A Gruesome, Grisly Gunpowder Plot

Not very far from where I used to live is one of the most peculiar buildings in Britain.

It stands on its own next to the railway line in the grounds of Rushton Hall, a grand historic house in Northamptonshire, now a posh hotel and spa. If you visit this **odd little building**, you might think it looks a bit like a witch's house, or something from a video game, or maybe an experiment by someone who is really good at maths. I say this because when you look closely you will see that everything about it comes in threes. It has three sides, three storeys, three gables with three pinnacles. If you think it looks like it is made out of triangles, you would not be the first. It is called the Triangular Lodge and has been mystifying people since it was built more than 400 years ago for a man called Sir Thomas Tresham.

Sir Thomas was Catholic at a time when that was a **very dangerous thing to be**. When the pope would not grant Henry VIII a divorce, Henry decided the English Church could do without the pope and he made himself the new boss instead. This went down very badly with faithful Catholics, including the Treshams. It put them in a tricky position, because if they stayed loyal to the pope then they would be disloyal to the king, and that meant TREASON. And for *that* you could easily end up fined, imprisoned or – gulp! – **executed**. This didn't just stop at Henry; when his daughter Elizabeth I became queen it was dangerous to mess with her too. Elizabeth was Protestant and she ended up sending Sir Thomas to prison for his Catholic beliefs.

If anything, prison made Sir Thomas even *more*

determined to stick to his beliefs, and on his release in 1593 he built the Triangular Lodge. He hoped Catholics would see it as a sort of riddle on the Holy Trinity – that's why it's all in threes – but it's actually a tribute to the old Catholic faith, carefully crafted with **secret codes**.

FACT BOX

Catholics and Protestants alike believe in the Holy Trinity – that there is one God in three equal forms, the father, the son and the Holy Spirit. But look out for the secret signs Sir Thomas added so a Catholic would recognise the lodge as a celebration of their faith.

If you visit the lodge today you might still find a whiff of secrets and danger. That's because the Treshams played an important part in a much bigger story, something that threatened to change the course of England's history forever.

A HEIST BEFORE BEDTIME

It began with Sir Thomas's son, Francis, who inherited the Triangular Lodge from his father in 1605, just a couple of years after Queen Elizabeth I died. King James I, who was also King of Scotland, was now on the throne of England and he was even more Protestant than Elizabeth was. And you *could* say Francis was even more Catholic than his father was. Like many English Catholics, he feared the whole country would become *even more* Protestant under James. What to do? Hatch a daring – or unbelievably reckless – **plot to get rid of the king**, of course.

The chief plotter was Robert Catesby, a Catholic landowner from neighbouring Warwickshire. Another was the one people still talk about today, Guy Fawkes. He's the original 'guy', the scarecrow we burn every Bonfire Night and remember to this day as the most notorious traitor in English history. (Fawkes was actually a soldier who had served with bravery and who was much loved by his friends.)

The plotters decided to take out King James I and the whole government by striking at the State Opening of

Parliament. This is a big ceremony held in the House of Lords every year, attended by lots of important people and led by the king or queen, who wears the crown and sits on the throne. Once all the dignitaries were settled in their places, the plotters would detonate a colossal charge of gunpowder they had hidden there, which would be enough to reduce the king and the government *and* Parliament to **nothing but dust and ashes**.

Then with the king out of the way the plotters planned to replace him on the throne with his nine-year-old daughter, Princess Elizabeth, who would be forced to rule as a Catholic. And so the plotters thought they would be remembered as England's saviours, for disposing of a 'fake' king, and reviving the true faith.

But history had other plans. And they are not remembered as saviours or heroes but as dreadful traitors who hatched one of the most horrible, heinous and hapless heists in history – the **Gunpowder Plot**.

There's an old story in Northamptonshire that the

Gunpowder Plot was hatched at the Triangular Lodge itself, a good choice of venue if you wanted to meet in secret and plan the assassination of a king. If you do ever visit, you'll see how easy it is to imagine the plotters whispering treason by the flickering light of lanterns and candles. Then imagine an owl hooting in the woods to add a bit of **spooky atmosphere** if you like . . .

I hate to spoil a story but, to be honest, most of the plotting was done at the pub, the old Duck and Drake off the Strand in London. We know that Catesby later asked Tresham for permission to use Rushton Hall, and for a large sum of money, but Tresham refused. Why? To answer to God for so terrible a deed as killing a king and the innocent people unlucky enough to be there could result in the eternal torments of hell, so he declined. However, he did give the plotters a small sum of money to help them with their plot. Perhaps he thought this modest involvement would be enough to spare him from blame. We shall see if he was right.

A GRUESOME, GRISLY GUNPOWDER PLOT

Meanwhile, the other plotters got on with their plotting, but the State Opening was delayed by an **outbreak of plague**, a dreadful disease that caused boils the size of apples to appear all over the body, which then filled with pus, and burst before death came. The king understandably decided to wait for it to pass before he got anywhere near a crowd and that gave the plotters time to rent a building next to Parliament. Some people say they dug a secret tunnel from it into Parliament's cellars, but I don't think that's right either. It's a nice story, but it's very unlikely they built a secret tunnel, for the simple reason that they just did not need to.

It is difficult to imagine this in our time, when you need your parent's password to get into an iPad let alone Parliament, but in those days it was not a secure building. People could just come and go: MPs, peers, officials, anyone with business there, servants, tradesmen, the curious, the curiouser – your Auntie Doris could have called in with her knitting. There were even shops and inns to cater to visitors. There *were* guards to keep order, if necessary, but no one checked people coming in and out, especially in the service parts of the building, like the kitchens and cellars and the storerooms, called undercrofts. No one thought anything was unusual when a man who worked for Thomas Percy rented the storeroom immediately next to the chamber of the House of Lords (one of the grandest

parts of Parliament, where the king's nobles met to make up laws). No one thought it was unusual either when dozens of kegs – small wooden barrels – arrived by the cartload and were stacked up there along with bundles of firewood (no health and safety in those days).

So no one bothered to look carefully enough at the kegs to discover that they **actually contained gunpowder**, enough to cause an explosion that would have destroyed anyone or anything within 50 metres (in case you are wondering, 50 metres is about the height of Nelson's Column or ten giraffes – take your pick). But did you know that gunpowder has a Best Before date? While the plotters were waiting for the delayed Opening of Parliament, the gunpowder got damp and no longer worked. Guy Fawkes, who knew his explosives, replaced it with fresh supplies.

Finally the date for the State Opening was fixed for 5 November, and by the end of October the plotters had finalised their plans. Everything was in place for the plotters to pull off the most daring, most dreadful, most devastating attack *ever* on the king and on Parliament. **And it might have gone to plan too. However . . .**

On 23 October, Tresham's relative Lord Monteagle, a Catholic who was not involved with the plot, was having a nice Sunday lunch at Hoxton, north of London, when he was handed an anonymous letter. The letter urged him to stay away from Parliament on the day of the State Opening because a 'terrible blow' would befall it. Lord Monteagle did not know what to make of this, so he took it to Lord Salisbury, the king's chief minister. The politics of state then – and now – was a leaky business, and news that Salisbury had seen a letter warning of a threat to Parliament soon reached Catesby. He immediately accused Tresham of having written it, which Tresham denied, but now he was even more anxious about the consequences of going ahead with the plot and he urged Catesby to **abort the mission**. Meanwhile, Salisbury, one of the wiliest politicians of his day, waited patiently until the king returned from hunting a few days later. He remembered that the king's own father had been assassinated in a huge gunpowder explosion (yes, indeed, but that is another story for another day) and he rightly guessed the king would go bananas when he showed him the letter. This is exactly what happened. So the king at once called a meeting of his councillors, and plans were made to search Parliament.

Now the plotters knew about the letter sent to Lord Monteagle and were beginning to get **nervous**. Why didn't they call it off? Perhaps they did not fully understand what was happening . . . perhaps now all the preparations were in place, aborting the mission was unthinkable . . . perhaps they were so committed to the cause they were prepared to take any risk. We do know that when the plotters met for the last time on Sunday 3 November they were urged to prepare themselves for 'the uttermost trial'.

Guy Fawkes took up his position alone in the undercroft and settled down for a long wait, with only the gunpowder, a fuse, something to light it with and a pocket watch for company. Then on the morning of Monday 4 November the door to the undercroft suddenly swung open and a group of men rushed in and cornered him. 'Who are you?' 'What's all this firewood for?' 'What are you doing here at this time of day?' I suppose they must have asked all those questions, but Fawkes kept his cool and said he was just a servant looking after it for his master. Then in surely one of the **worst examples of detective work in history**, they merely said, 'Oh, OK then,' or something like that, and left. Luckily (though unluckily for Fawkes), when one of them reported this to Lord Monteagle he put two and two together. So later that night a group of men, led by Thomas Knyvet, returned to the cellar and that's how Fawkes, now dressed for his escape, holding a lantern and very suspiciously in possession of matches and kindling (small pieces of wood used to start a fire), was caught red-handed. 'Who are you?' they asked. 'John Johnson,' replied Fawkes, which definitely lacked imagination, but to be fair it must have been a terrifying moment for he would have

— A GRUESOME, GRISLY GUNPOWDER PLOT —

known very well that the penalty for **High Treason in England in 1605 was death** (and a very unpleasant one at that).

On the morning of 5 November 1605, the day of the State Opening of Parliament, Fawkes was brought before the king. He claimed bravely that he had acted alone, which impressed James, but not enough to spare him from the **torturer**. The king commanded that Fawkes be taken to the Tower of London, where he was questioned by the Attorney General, Sir William Coke, who had some terrible tools at his disposal to encourage prisoners to tell him what he wanted to hear. We don't know exactly what happened to Fawkes, but he was probably put on the rack. This was a wooden frame raised off the floor with two large rollers at either end. The unlucky prisoner would be laid on it and his arms strapped by leather cords or chains to the top roller, with his legs strapped to the bottom roller. These would then be slowly wound in opposite directions so that arms and legs were gradually stretched and stretched and stretched until they were sometimes **pulled apart**. It caused unbelievable pain, so intense that even the bravest of its victims eventually confessed — to anything, pretty much — just to make it stop. You can see Guy Fawkes' confession today; it is kept at the National Archives in Kew. He didn't write it all out himself; a secretary did that. He just signed it in a faint and wobbly hand, which tells you something about what he must have endured.

His was not the only wobbly signature at the bottom of a confession. Over the next few weeks others were arrested too, and brought to the Tower. By the middle of January, Coke had interrogated enough men to make a case for the prosecution, and a trial was set for Westminster Hall on 26 January 1606. Facing the Lord Chief Justice were eight of the plotters, Ambrose Rookwood, Thomas and Robert Wintour, Thomas Bates, John Grant, Robert Keyes, Sir Everard Digby and Guy Fawkes, who were brought by barge from the Tower (actually, Bates was not considered grand enough for the Tower of London and was brought from a different prison). **The charge was High Treason**, the evidence against them was powerful and the judges did not struggle to find them guilty (the king was among the spectators, which may have encouraged them to reach their decision).

They were all sentenced to death, which

was bad enough, but the death reserved for traitors was one of the worst an executioner could devise – they would be hanged, drawn and quartered. The condemned men would be strapped to a frame, which was hitched to a horse and then dragged through the streets of London to the boos of the huge crowds. They were then handed over to the executioner, who stripped them of their clothes and hanged them from a gallows until they were half dead. Then they were cut down, and as they revived, the executioner took a butcher's knife and cut bits off them. Then they were sliced open, their guts pulled out, then he tore out their probably still beating hearts and threw them on a fire. Finally they were beheaded, their arms and legs chopped off, and their mangled bits sent to the four corners of the kingdom to be put on display and pecked at by birds.

Why such a cruel punishment? Partly to warn off any others from thinking they might try to overthrow the king, and partly to put on an unforgettable show of the king's power – to prove he had the power of life and death, and a death so awful it would give nightmares to anyone who witnessed it.

On the last two days of January 1606, in freezing weather, the condemned eight suffered the punishment; four by St Paul's Cathedral and four in front of the building they had plotted to blow up. Guy Fawkes was one of those last four, but he cheated the bloodthirsty crowds by jumping off the scaffold when the noose was fastened around his neck, so it broke, and he died instantly rather than undergo the torments the others endured.

In fact, he was not the only one of the plotters to cheat the executioner. Robert Catesby, the ringleader, never even got to trial. When news of the plot broke, he wasn't in London but in Staffordshire, where he had planned to lead the rebellion that would replace James with Princess Elizabeth. He took refuge in Holbeche House near Birmingham, and there with some fellow plotters he tried to dry some damp gunpowder in front of the fire to make a last stand. It ignited, however, and they were engulfed in flames. Catesby survived, but not for long. When the Sheriff of Worcester arrived at Holbeche House with **200 men** there was an epic gun battle and Catesby **was shot dead.**

And what of Francis Tresham? He was also named as one of the plotters by Guy Fawkes under torture, and was taken to the Tower of London. But before he could be brought before a court he fell ill with strangury, a condition that leaves you bursting for a wee but unable to go. It lasted for days until, after suffering agonies, infection set in and he died. It spared the living man the executioner, but not his corpse. After the other plotters were convicted, Tresham's body was dug up and beheaded anyway; **his head was stuck on a pike** and put on display in Northampton next to Catesby's.

There were celebrations all over the kingdom that the conspiracy had failed, and a special church service was invented to give thanks that the plot was foiled and England would stay Protestant. Today in Britain we are free to worship in any way we wish, but we still remember the Gunpowder Plot on Bonfire Night with fireworks, the burning of the guy, and the annual ritual of trying to write rude words in the darkness with sparklers. 'Remember, remember the fifth of November, gunpowder, treason and plot!' we chanted when we were kids as the flames took hold. I remember celebrating Bonfire Night one year in Rushton. The fireworks burst in the night sky, lighting up Rushton Hall with its Triangular Lodge throwing jagged shadows against the flashes of light. And the more imaginative among us maybe saw for a split second some ghostly men in cloaks and tall hats with wide brims, huddled together plotting to kill a king.

The Maple Syrup Mystery

I was woken up early one morning by my phone ringing. It was a friend of mine and he sounded agitated. 'What's the matter?' I asked sleepily. 'I have an emergency!' he replied.

Suddenly wide awake, I said, 'What do you need?' 'Maple syrup!' was the answer.

Now, my friend is Canadian and he loves maple syrup. Not just any maple syrup but the best maple syrup – grade one – and he's very fussy about it indeed. He lives in Montreal, where the supermarkets are full of grade-one maple syrup, but he was spending the summer in England near where I live. He had only arrived the night before but when he woke up the next morning he discovered he'd forgotten to bring a bottle of maple syrup from home. What was he supposed to put on his pancakes for breakfast if he didn't have any maple syrup?!

So my friend put on his slippers and went round to the corner shop, but they only had ordinary maple syrup and he wasn't going to stoop to that. And that's why he phoned me. Fortunately, I knew where he could get a bottle of grade-one maple syrup so I dropped him a pin, he quickly called a taxi and off he went to fetch some in his slippers and dressing gown.

Why would someone go to such trouble for a dribble of tree sap (as that's what maple syrup actually is)?

I don't know; it's not my favourite syrup, to be honest, but the good stuff is so highly valued by people who love it that **just one barrel can cost as much as a PlayStation 5 Pro!** The best stuff comes from the red maple tree, which grows in the forests of Québec, Canada. It was harvested by the people of the First Nations, who

THE MAPLE SYRUP MYSTERY

lived in what we now call Canada long before the arrival of settlers from Europe. Today C$1.5bn worth of it is sold to countries around the world including Britain (fortunately for my friend). It's so important that the Canadian flag even has a big red maple leaf on it!

So how do you collect maple syrup to ship around the world? Well, first you have to wait for the right season, which is around the end of winter. This is 'sugar weather', when the nights are below freezing and the days are mild. This means the sap will flow when it's tapped. To do that, the growers cut a notch in the bark of the maple tree and into that stick a little metal tap with a special metal pail beneath it to collect the sap that seeps out. The sap is then taken to special processing plants called sugar shacks, and boiled to reduce the water content. And there's your syrup. A single tree can produce about **50 litres of raw sap** in one season. Maple syrup season can be longer or shorter depending on the weather, so producers never know quite how much sap they're going to get each year. Their customers are going to want their syrup whatever the weather though, so how can they make sure there's enough to go round when the season is short?

The answer is that they store syrup in special warehouses from a previous year when they had more than they needed. That way there's always enough for their customers. It's called the **Global Strategic Reserve**, which is quite a mouthful – a bit like the syrup itself. And when you think about it, because maple syrup sells for a high price there's a lot of money's worth of syrup in one of those warehouses! If just one of those warehouses has room for 90,000 barrels, each containing 45 gallons of syrup, then warehouses that are full have a whopping **C$400m worth of maple syrup** just sitting there waiting to be shipped to the shops.

Four hundred million dollars?!? It's a mind-boggling mountain of marketable maple. That's about the equivalent of £200m and almost what Paris Saint-Germain paid for the famous footballer Neymar! And it's not only pancake fans who salivate at the thought of that. Robbers do too. For what they can see is C$400m lying around conveniently in barrels, just asking to be pinched, and unlike like Fort Knox – where the United States government keeps all its gold bars, protected by an army brigade – there are no troops around to guard it. As it turns out there were indeed some stealthy scoundrels with maple mischief in mind, and in 2011 a **massive Maple Syrup Heist** would begin.

One of the heist ringleaders was Avik Caron, whose wife owned a warehouse at Saint-Louis-de-Blandford that the Federation of Québec Maple Syrup Producers had hired to store maple syrup in after a bumper harvest. Because it was being stored there temporarily, security was even lighter than normal; no alarms, no cameras, no security guards (and anyway Avik could go in and out as he pleased unbeknown to his wife). Avik got together with a syrup producer called Richard Vallières – who was really the mastermind of the heist and had fallen out with the Federation very badly – as well as a syrup dealer called Étienne St-Pierre and a trucker called Sébastien Jutras.

These four were actually just the core of the gang, as others were involved in the heist too, but it was these four men who came up with a simple plan: to run a real maple syrup business, which meant they could all come and go from the warehouse without raising suspicion. Then they would help themselves to the stored barrels of sap, take them to New Brunswick where they had their own sugar shack, siphon out the sap and refill the barrels with water. They would then put the water-filled barrels back in the warehouse. Meanwhile, the syrup they had made in their sugar shack was sold on the black market (a network of people who buy and sell stuff illegally) by Richard Vallières, who was what is known as a barrel-roller – someone who produces and sells syrup without going through the Federation. The Federation is in charge of how much maple syrup gets sold, so if you are a maple syrup seller it is very naughty not to notify them of what you are doing. And if you are caught you will be fined. So Richard was careful to sell the syrup at the normal price rather than a suspiciously low one. This way he was less likely to get dobbed in.

The plan was put into action and before 2012 was out the gang had stolen nearly 10,000 barrels containing nearly 3,000 tonnes of the stuff. This is the equivalent weight of

300 T-rexes, or 4,000 cows, or 1,500 cars, or the giant roof over Centre Court at Wimbledon. If you prefer to think of it as liquid then that's about what it would take to **fill an Olympic swimming pool**. (Don't try to break any records by swimming in maple syrup though – it would be slow and very sticky.)

That amount in syrup is also C$20m dollars of cash. Twenty million *easy* dollars because the gang could access the warehouses without anyone noticing anything, so they pretty much helped themselves to as much syrup as they wanted. All they needed to do was turn up at the warehouse after the workers had all gone home, forklift the barrels on to their lorry and drive it off to their sugar shack where they would siphon, boil, refill, siphon again, then fill them with water, take them back to the warehouse and put the barrel back in the pile. Then they would take that luscious lucrative syrup and sell it for loads of lovely lolly (that's slang for '*sweet* money'). The gang always took small batches so they didn't rouse any suspicions, then trucked it as far west as Ontario and as far south as Vermont and New Hampshire, across the border with America. There, they sold it to distributors who didn't even know it had been stolen.

It was so easy that after a year the gang got complacent, which usually means you're about to **make a mistake**. Rather than truck the stolen sap to their sugar shack to siphon out the syrup, they just did it in the warehouse where it was stored, saving themselves a job. Then they stopped bothering to refill the barrels with water, instead replacing empty unfilled barrels back in the stack.

And this is what got them caught. Every year a Federation official was sent to inspect the barrels in their warehouses. The gang wasn't worried about this, because one plain white barrel looks pretty much like another plain white barrel. They made sure they never took a barrel away without replacing it so what was there to notice? But this inspector, Michel Gauvreau, was a very thorough man and he decided he would actually climb up the stack of barrels to check all was in order. A full barrel weighed 270 kg and was pretty solid if it was stacked up with other barrels, which made it easier to climb on (though I would strongly recommend not climbing on stacks of barrels even if they are full unless you are a qualified maple syrup inspector). But an empty one was definitely not stable, and when Michel climbed on it, it gave way, causing Michel to nearly fall. **It could have killed him if he had.**

The game was up. The Federation sent a team to inspect the barrel. That's when they realised it had been emptied, so they ordered a check on them all. At first the gang had tried to cover their tracks, sticking fake labels on the barrels to divert suspicion, but as time went by and they got sloppy, they didn't bother. This made it easy for the inspectors to see which barrels had been tampered with. They had also started to use the wrong kind of forklift to move them, which left obvious scratches on the barrels, and on top of that the water they had filled them with caused some of the barrels to rust. The Federation soon discovered the

―――― THE MAPLE SYRUP MYSTERY ――――

scale of the theft and the shocking truth: that an Olympic swimming pool-sized booty of maple syrup had been nicked from under their noses!

The Federation called the Sûreté du Québec, the local police, which launched its largest investigation ever. They interviewed 300 people, knocked on forty doors with search warrants and even involved US Customs and Immigration, as well as the best-dressed police force in the world, the Royal Canadian Mounted Police. **Do you know about the Mounties?** They are the national police force in Canada and are famous for riding around on horses in scarlet uniforms and cool hats. Four of their officers led the funeral procession of Queen Elizabeth II through London in 2022. It is said that when they go after suspects the Mounties ALWAYS succeed in catching them, so with them on the case, the noose finally began to tighten around the robbers.

However, it was not a straightforward case. The police now had to find the **stolen syrup**. It is not easy to tell

where the syrup you pour over your pancake has actually come from; you cannot trace it to an individual producer or distributor, so the police investigation took ages. They even used **new technology** that shone UV light through syrup to reveal if it had been messed about with. Eventually they managed to recover 70% of the stolen syrup. But four years went by before they brought charges against the gang. Sébastien Jutras, the gang's trucker, was charged with transporting the stolen syrup. He said he didn't know it was stolen, but the court convicted him and he ended up doing eight months in prison. Étienne St-Pierre, the syrup seller, got two years in prison and was fined nearly a million dollars. He also said he had no idea the syrup was stolen. Avik Caron, whose wife owned the Federation's warehouse, was sentenced to five years in prison and fined more than a million dollars.

They threw the book at Richard Vallières. He was accused of being the ringleader but defended himself by saying he had been threatened by organised criminals who told him if he did not steal the syrup for them, they would kill his family. The court did not believe him and in 2017 he was sentenced to EIGHT years in prison and was fined **more than 9 million dollars** (they also convicted his dad, Raymond Vallières, for possession of stolen syrup, and he got two years in jail!).

Nine million dollars is a HUGE fine, but remember C$18m of stolen syrup had gone missing, and the money must have gone to someone. Richard was given ten years to pay it back or face another six years in prison. His lawyers thought this was too severe a sentence. They went back to court and this time the judge decided he need only pay back what he admitted he had made from the heist – the fine was reduced from C$9m to C$1m. But the Federation didn't like that so they took him back to court *again*, and this time the judge said he *did* have to pay the C$9m after all!

The whole **sticky affair** did not end there. A TV documentary was made about the heist and the story gripped the public's imagination and also Hollywood's, where in 2024 a TV series based on the story called *The Sticky* was made. It was not a faithful telling of the story though – it turned Richard into a woman called Ruth Landry, a disenchanted and very sweary maple syrup grower with a husband in a coma. None of that was true but it was a big hit with viewers.

Why do people like this story so much? For a number of reasons, I think. Lots of people, like my friend, love maple syrup and are interested in it just because of that. I'm very fond of a pickled onion and if there were a heist involving disgruntled onion picklers I would be interested too, wouldn't you? I also don't think many people know just how valuable maple syrup is, and maybe a part of us thinks it's ludicrous that C$400m worth of the stuff was just left lying around in barrels practically waiting to be pinched. Perhaps we like the ingenuity and the cheek of the robbers, small producers who saw an opportunity and took it, ending up C$18m richer (though not for long). Mostly I think we like stories about little people standing up to big people, like Robin Hood and his Merry Men standing up to the Sheriff of Nottingham. But the Maple Syrup Robbers did not take from the rich to give to the poor, they took from the rich to enrich themselves, and they did so in a way that broke the law of the land. And when *that* happens, you can end up in jail.

When I was a little boy I realised that the Millennium (which is when the twentieth century became the twenty-first century) would happen when I was thirty-eight. I had no idea what being thirty-eight would be like, although I thought we would probably get around on hover scooters, and robots would tidy our bedrooms. What I was most looking forward to was the opening of my kindergarten's **time capsule**, a box of bits and bobs we buried in the school garden when I was a little boy of six. Well, the Millennium arrived and hover scooters and room tidying robots were still some way off, and I had completely forgotten about my kindergarten time capsule. I only remembered it just now and have no idea if it was dug up. In fact, I can't even remember what was put inside.

But I do remember what we did when the Millennium finally arrived. The government in London decided to mark this **once-in-a-thousand years** moment by building a giant dome on some derelict land on a bend of the River Thames in East London. The Millennium Dome was like a giant circus tent in a way, only instead of clowns and trapeze artists to entertain us (actually there were trapeze artists on the first night) there were lots of different 'zones' inside that you could visit. The idea was to explore the big themes about life in Britain and the world at this moment in time, but because this was all decided by politicians rather than people who put on shows, there were endless committees trying to agree on what to put in there. Like most things designed by committees it didn't really work because **everybody had different ideas**. There was a Faith Zone that caused representatives of different religions to fall out over who got more space and who got less; a zone about Earth's fragile environment was situated next to a display sponsored by a car manufacturer. Some zones were actually quite cool: the Body Zone was made of two giant bodies you could walk round. I remember you went in through one of the elbows.

The grand opening of the Millennium Dome took place on New Year's Eve, and thousands of VIPs were invited to join the queen and the prime minister there to sing 'Auld Lang Syne' (the song you often sing at midnight to mark the start of a new year – look it up if you've never heard of it). As it happened, on the night unfortunately lots of them got stuck at security checks at the tube station and ended up seeing in the new Millennium while queuing outside in the cold and the dark, which was disappointing. In fact a lot of people thought there was something a bit disappointing about the whole Millennium Dome thing.

Something that did not disappoint, though, was the Money Zone, and that was thanks to an amazing display of diamonds put on by De Beers, **the biggest diamond-mining company in the world**. They had in their vaults some of the most dazzling, glittery, sparkly, flashy and EXPENSIVE diamonds of all. When visitors saw them they went 'ooh', some went 'aah', and maybe 'ooh' *and* 'aah' when they saw the star of the show, the super-precious Millennium Star, a flawless white diamond, the second-largest of its kind in the world, weighing in at more than **200 carats**. Most diamonds are tiny, but this looks like something that's fallen off a chandelier. It was found in Zaire (now the Democratic Republic of Congo) by a miner working for De Beers in 1990. Diamonds dug out of the earth don't look anything like the sparkly things in the jeweller's; they look more like gravel, and who would pay **a million quid for that?** They have to be carefully cut and polished before someone would want to pay lots of money for them, and because this diamond was so big,

De Beers took it to the world's leading diamond cutter, Nir Livnat.

It is EXTREMELY difficult to cut diamonds, because they are one of the hardest-known substances in nature, so you need very special tools, and one badly judged cut can wreck the whole thing. Also, to get the best-finished diamond you have to lose a lot of the original diamond lump it is cut from. Those 200 carats were originally 770 carats, so the Millennium Star is just under a quarter of its original weight. But even so it was worth around £500m in today's money. **That's half a billion quid.**

So De Beers made the Millennium Star the centrepiece of their diamond display, and to make everyone do another **'ooh'** or maybe an **'aah'**, or both, they shone a laser through it so it sent sparkles all round the inside of the enormous Dome!

The day after the opening night, New Year's Day 2000, the Millennium Dome opened to the public. Queues of people filed into the Money Zone and into De Beers' super-secure diamond exhibit. There, in a hexagonal steel vault, behind thick glass, the Millennium Star sparkled on a stand surrounded by rare blue diamonds on smaller stands. It made the display look like a galaxy of stars. And, as expected, everyone oohed and aahed, and *some* people liked it so much they came back to see it again, but these people were looking at the Millennium Star for a different reason.

Lee Wenham, Raymond Betson and William Cockram kept returning to see the Millennium Star, not because they were fans of exceptionally rare and dazzling gems for their beauty but because they are so expensive. They were members of one of the **most notorious and organised armed robber gangs in the country**, a gang which also included Terry Millman, Aldo Ciarrocchi, Robert Adams, Kevin Meredith and James Hurley.

To them, the Millennium Star looked like just about the richest picking imaginable for any ambitious robber, and they had a history when it came to ambitious robberies. Actually they had already had a busy Millennium year. In February 2000 some of the gang had nearly pulled off a notorious raid on a bank van carrying £10m in cash. The van's route took it down Nine Elms Lane near the South Bank of the River Thames in London. When it got there the robbers blocked off both ends of the lane, so the van was trapped. Then another member of the gang arrived driving a lorry loaded with Christmas trees. This was a curious cargo for February, but what was really unusual was that the Christmas trees concealed **a giant steel spike** welded on to the lorry, its point sticking out at the back. The robbers planned to use it as a sort of battering ram, by reversing the lorry into the van and using the spike to force open the rear doors. They would then grab the money and escape in a powerboat waiting for them on the Thames. A daring and ingenious plan, foiled, however, thanks to an impatient London motorist. When the robbers parked the Christmas tree lorry nearby to get ready for the raid it blocked a man in a car who had somewhere to go. When he went to argue with the driver of the lorry, he found no one there (the driver was too busy holding up the van at this point) so in a fit of temper the motorist took the keys from the lorry (which the robber had left in the ignition) to teach him a lesson for blocking his car in. Imagine the frustration the robbers must have felt when they went to fetch the battering ram lorry to break open the van and found **their keys had been taken**. There was nothing they could do but get in the boat and head down the Thames empty-handed.

'The best-laid plans o' mice an' men gang aft agley,' said Robert Burns, the great Scottish poet who people have been misunderstanding for two hundred years. It means that anyone can mess things up, even London's most daring robber gang. But they did not give up. Later that year, in the summer, they had another go, this time in Aylesford in Kent. Using a similar method, they stopped a security van carrying more than £8m. This time they threatened the terrified driver and guard with explosive devices that they stuck on to the side of the van before driving their giant spike into the back doors. They were just about to help themselves to the money when the police, who had been alerted by the public, arrived. The gang members fired sawn-off shotguns, fortunately without hurting anyone, before they jumped empty-handed into a van that drove at top speed to the banks of the River Medway. There, another speedboat was waiting for them. They jumped into it and got away. When the police examined the giant spike, they found the robbers had left a message for them that said, 'Persistent, aren't we?' They also found that the explosive devices fixed to the van were **tinned steak and kidney pies** painted green and fitted with **flashing lights**.

When the Kent police recovered the vans the gangs had used in the raid, they found they had a connection with Lee Wenham's family. Traces of saliva from Lee Wenham had been found at the scene of the crime, so now the police knew he was involved. And with the Wenhams being the

Wenhams they realised it wouldn't be long before this ambitious crime dynasty hatched another plan.

They were right about that, so this is where our story returns to the Millennium Dome and the sparkling De Beers diamond . . .

So, as we know, among the visitors to the Dome were Lee Wenham, Raymond Betson and William Cockram, who seemed to like it so much they came back again and again – and every time they revisited the diamond exhibition, which was clearly their favourite. The police were watching them and it was thought unlikely they were interested in jewellery for fashion reasons. None of them looked like they would be seen swanning around in a tiara and they seemed much more interested in the security arrangements than in the diamonds themselves. It was also observed that their visits coincided with high tide on the Thames, a tide that would be handy if they were planning, say, **a getaway on a speedboat**.

Serious crime, especially that involving armed robbers,

is dealt with by the Flying Squad in the Metropolitan Police. It would be nice to think this was made up of police officers with jet packs zooming around the capital, but actually it's just a nickname they got for moving quickly to catch the **most dangerous criminals** in town. With the Flying Squad on board, it wasn't long before the police realised that not only were gang members visiting the Dome more frequently in September and taking detailed videos of their visits, but another man, also associated with the gang, was seen putting a speedboat through its paces off the Kent shore.

When October came round, the Flying Squad issued a couple of red alerts that the raid was imminent, but on the first attempt the speedboat failed and on the second the tide was too low for a river getaway to work. But by 5 November – remember that date; it is the same as the Gunpowder Plot – the police had worked out the raid would mostly likely take place two days later, on the 7th. The Flying Squad initiated 'Operation Magician', a very big operation indeed, with 200 officers involved. This included forty from the Specialist Firearms Command, some of them disguised as the Dome's regular security guards and others in full tactical gear positioned behind a false wall at the end of a service tunnel. The trap was set, but what would the raid actually look like?

The answer came with the distant sound of a diesel engine, the rattle of gears and the squeak of machinery, as a bright-yellow JCB digger approached the Millennium Dome. Nothing particularly noteworthy about a digger in London – well, not until you noticed that the four 'builders' on board were wearing **gas masks and body armour** and drove straight through a barrier. They then

headed to the wall of the Dome. Why was the digger driving at the wall? Because on the other side was the vault where the Millennium Star surrounded by its rare blue diamond friends was twinkling temptingly in the spotlights!

The police watching this realised what was going to happen. Remember the giant battering ram hidden inside a lorry-load of Christmas trees? Why unlock a door when you can knock it down? **With a mighty crash** the JCB punched a hole through the wall, and the gang members sprang into action, throwing smoke bombs to give cover, and wielding ammonia spray, nail guns and sledgehammers with which they surrounded the steel vault (the vault happened to be closed that day for cleaning). Once in, they attacked the security glass protecting the diamonds. And as they battered at it with sledgehammers and nail guns it gave way and **the diamonds were in their grasp**.

But in fact the robbers had put themselves firmly in the *cops'* grasp. Within seconds the four JCB drivers were overpowered by armed officers, who wrestled them to the floor. Outside, another unit arrested a fifth gang member who was waiting in a speedboat on the river. And a third unit arrested a man monitoring radio frequencies nearby. It was all over in minutes. While this was happening, officers in Kent moved against Lee Wenham, who was nicked in his van. They then swooped and arrested *another* six men at the Wenhams' farm, the gang's HQ. Yes, the cops copped the lot and the robbers copped not a lot.

There were a few loose ends that needed tying up but that was done in just a few days. So the gang was in custody, and while the Money Zone was temporarily closed, the Dome reopened and the diamonds carried on twinkling undisturbed until the Millennium year was up. After that, the Dome was converted into a venue where you can now go and see different sorts of stars, like Ed Sheeran and Taylor Swift, twinkling in their own way.

The robbers were put before a magistrate and remanded in custody (which means sent to jail) to wait for the police to put a case together that could be tried in court. The robbers also had to get lawyers to defend themselves. It was all such a complicated process that **it took a year before the trial began** in the Central Criminal Court in London, the Old Bailey. This is where some of the most famous and infamous trials in history have taken place.

The judge was Mr Justice Coombes, who had the jury sworn in and the prisoners brought into the dock. Of the seven gang members only six appeared, for Terry Millman unfortunately had died of cancer while awaiting trial. Among the remaining robbers on trial was William Cockram, who complained that security at the Dome was woefully inadequate and nothing could have been easier than breaking in and taking the diamonds. When asked if the gang posed a serious threat to the public he said, 'No, because a trip to the Dome was such a boring day out it was only ever half empty.' What about the nail gun? 'To be used to break the glass.' The ammonia? 'To destroy any DNA evidence.' There was the usual dance of accusation and denial when some of the gang pointed the finger at others to get themselves off the hook. There was lots of evidence heard about how carefully they had laid their plans; premises were rented in which to keep their kit; tens of thousands of pounds had been invested in the heist, including nearly four grand to buy a speedboat in the name of 'T. Diamond'. Everyone sniggered at this detail. They sniggered again when the leading investigating officer said his suspicions were raised when they saw the robbers returning to check out the display. 'No one goes to the Dome twice,' he said.

The cops also had to give evidence. There was a question about why they had not arrested the robbers before the mayhem unfolded at the Dome. They said they thought it would be better to arrest as many of the gang as possible in one go, while they were actually busy breaking into the display case. And it was because of the police that the vault had been closed 'for cleaning' that day so they could be sure there were no members of the public there when the raid happened.

It took three months for the twelve men and women of the jury to hear all the evidence. They then spent a whole week deciding their verdict . . . or *not* quite deciding their verdict. The best they could manage was 10–2 in favour of guilty, which the judge accepted. When it came to sentencing, he said, 'You played for very high stakes, and you must have known perfectly well what the penalty would be if your enterprise did not succeed.' Of those who were convicted and sentenced, Betson and Cockram, the ringleaders, got eighteen years. Aldo Ciarrocchi and Robert Adams got fifteen years. Kevin Meredith was cleared of two charges and got five years.

During those long years of imprisonment I wonder if they ever tortured themselves by thinking how near they had got to the Millennium Star and its glittering hoard, and hundreds of millions of pounds in swag? They were literally only centimetres away as they sledgehammered and nail-gunned the fracturing glass protecting the diamonds. Perhaps they could almost SMELL them (well, probably not because diamonds don't smell of anything as far as I know).

How near they got! Actually it turns out, they were not near at all. When the cops told De Beers a raid was imminent, they replaced all the diamonds with glass fakes. If the robbers had managed to snatch them and make their speedboat getaway after all, their swag would only have added up to **a few quid**.

A Perfectly Preposterous Princess Prank

I was in the city of Bath yesterday, where I visited the ballroom at the Guildhall. Inside there is a magnificent room with elegant plaster, portraits of lords and ladies, and three incredible chandeliers sparkling overhead. Two hundred or so years ago, splendid dances were held here to entertain the smartest members of society. One of the most spectacular of all was held in the early summer of 1817 in honour of **a mysterious young woman**. She was dressed in silks and wearing a magnificent headdress adorned with peacock feathers. She was the celebrated

— A HEIST BEFORE BEDTIME —

Princess Caraboo of the mysterious island of Javasu, or at least that's what she said.

The story begins on the Thursday before Easter that year, a day traditionally known in England as Maundy Thursday. On this day, it's the custom for the king or queen to visit a cathedral and give to locals a purse of silver coins called **Maundy money** – a penny for each year of the monarch's age (in other words a penny for each year the king or queen has been alive). It used to be a dole of cash given to the poor but these days it's ceremonial, given to people who have for many years done **amazing things** for their communities. The purse is made of soft leather, and the money is specially made at the Royal Mint, which makes all the coins we use every day. The Maundy money is different; the coins are made of silver and are worth one, two, three and four pence, and although you can use them to buy something in a shop, you would most likely get a funny look from the shopkeeper if you tried.

On this particular Maundy Thursday in 1817, there

was a royal visitor to the little village of Almondsbury near Bristol. However, it wasn't King George III, who was king of England at the time, and instead of a purse of Maundy money this 'royal' had only a dodgy sixpence.

And so that's where the story begins – in Almondsbury on the evening of Maundy Thursday, 3 April in 1817, when a young woman arrived dressed in black and wearing a shawl of black and red. Nothing particularly unusual about that – but her outfit was topped off with a splendid headdress, a sort of turban, wound round her thick black hair. This was an unusual thing to wear in Almondsbury in 1817, so the woman stood out immediately when she was seen walking up and down the street near the pub, called The Bowl Inn (still there today), and the church, called St Mary's (also still there). The woman, who was **waving her hands around** and looking **very uncertain** of where she was and what she should do, eventually knocked on the door of the village cobbler. When the cobbler opened the door, it soon became clear the woman couldn't speak any English, and the cobbler and his wife couldn't speak whatever her language was either. But she mimed eating and drinking and so they gave her some bread and some milk. When she then mimed falling asleep, they realised she was also looking for shelter. The cobbler's wife wasn't keen on letting her stay there, for the hopeful houseguest was carrying nothing but a little bundle containing only a bar of soap and a few coins, including a sixpence that didn't look right.

So the cobbler and his wife took the woman to the Overseer of the Poor, a local person whose responsibility in those days was to decide what to do with **people who**

didn't have any money or anywhere to go. Only *he* did not know what to do with her either, so he took her to see the local magistrate, Mr Worrall, who lived at the big house nearby called Knole Park.

The Overseer thought Mr Worrall's servant, who was Greek, might be able to understand this strange woman who spoke in a language he could not. Alas, when Mr Worrall summoned his servant, he couldn't make out a word of what she was saying either, but before Mr Worrall could send her away, his wife Elizabeth, an American who perhaps sympathised with someone so far away from home, decided to take her to the village inn. There she arranged for her to have a bed for the night and breakfast in the morning. Then Mrs Worrall sat her down and said that if she were not what she appeared to be, but just a swindler trying to con a charitable woman out of a meal and somewhere to sleep, she should confess it right now and no more would be said about it. But the girl just smiled sweetly, apparently unable to understand what she was saying. 'I am Mrs Worrall,' said Mrs Worrall, pointing at herself. 'WORRALL!' 'Caraboo,' said the young woman, pointing at herself. 'CARABOO!'

Another clue to her identity was revealed when the young woman saw a pineapple in the patterned wallpaper. She pointed at it and said, 'Nanas', a word that means pineapple in some languages. Maybe *that* would help them work out where she was from. Then when she saw some Chinese scenes illustrated in a book she got even more excited – maybe she was from somewhere out east? But these clues weren't enough for Mr Worrall, I'm afraid, who simply decided she was a beggar and should appear before the magistrates' court at Bristol on a charge of vagrancy. In those harsh days if you were unlucky enough to be homeless you were labelled a 'vagrant' and considered to be breaking the law. And so the **mysterious woman** was put in the poorhouse, where food and shelter was provided in exchange for back-breaking work and which was more like a prison than a refuge.

Poor Caraboo – things weren't looking good for her as she was locked up and awaiting trial; but then all at once **her luck changed**. For the tender-hearted Mrs Worrall managed to persuade her husband that she should be released from the poorhouse and accommodated instead at her husband's offices in the city until they could find out more about her.

There, various people were asked to visit the curious Caraboo to see if they could work out her language; Bristol was then the busiest port in England after London so there were lots of merchants and sailors from different lands passing through. One of those sailors was Portuguese; he was brought to Caraboo and *finally* someone could understand her – or at least half understand her. For she was apparently speaking a hotchpotch of languages the sailor recognised from the coast of Sumatra – **an island in what we now call Indonesia**. And so the sailor was able to give an outline of her story. It was quite the tale too . . .

Caraboo was no vagrant, but a princess from the island of Javasu, she said. She had been kidnapped by pirates who had gone halfway round the world before they sailed up the Bristol Channel. When she finally saw her chance to escape, she jumped overboard and swam to the shore. And *that* was how she had found herself wandering in a daze round a little village called Almondsbury.

A princess! From the far-off East Indies! Kidnapped by pirates! Mrs Worrall at once invited her back to stay at Knole Park, and even Mr Worrall was persuaded when she related this dramatic tale. In quite the turnaround she was immediately treated not like a beggar but like **visiting royalty**, which as far as the Worralls were concerned she now was. Word of the **mysterious princess** staying at Knole Park soon spread across the district and then the county, and then even beyond that, and before long curious visitors were queuing up to meet her.

It just so happened that one of the Worralls' friends was a merchant who had travelled widely in the Far East, so they asked him to talk to Caraboo to see if he could uncover any more of her story. Using his knowledge of Chinese languages as well as various dictionaries and accounts from other travellers, he did indeed manage to piece together a fuller story of Princess Caraboo's life and adventures. **It was a story that did not disappoint.**

The princess was the daughter of a Chinese nobleman who ruled the faraway island of Javasu. Her mother had unfortunately been eaten by cannibals, and if that were not enough tragedy to endure, more came when the princess was seized by pirates while walking in her garden one day. The pirates dragged her to their ship, bound her and set sail. And the last she saw of her native land was her father standing on the beach in despair. But that wasn't all . . . When the pirates got to port, they sold her to another trader who sailed yet further round the world, eventually taking her to Bristol, which is where her **daring escape took place** and how she arrived in the Worralls' lives. On hearing this, the Worralls were deeply moved, and to make her feel even more welcome at Knole – and maybe because they felt a *little* bit guilty that they had originally had her locked up – they kitted her out with a wardrobe worthy of an Eastern princess.

They engaged the portrait painter Edward Bird to paint her, and you can still see the picture today at the Bristol Museum and Art Gallery. The painting shows a beautiful young woman in strappy sandals wearing a shimmering gown in yellow silk and an extravagant headdress made up of a turban decorated with peacock feathers. In the background is a pagoda – a multi-storey traditional Chinese building. By the way, if you *do* visit this museum, check out the mummies, the Banksy, and Alfred the stuffed gorilla too! But back to the Worralls . . .

Caraboo turned out to be a brilliant guest, dazzling everyone she met. She was a crack shot with a bow and arrow, a decent swordswoman and, like lots of us today, she loved wild swimming, jumping into the lake at Knole whenever she felt like it (only she did it naked, which rather startled her hosts).

The princess drank only water and tea, ate curry and once cut the head off a live pigeon before eating it. The Worralls also noticed that under her turban the princess had peculiar marks on her head, some sort of tattoos or symbols – a sign of her noble birth, or her religion, perhaps. She certainly seemed religious; when she wasn't practising the arts of war and swimming in the lake, she was climbing trees, where she sat in the branches praying to a god she called Allatallah.

Soon, stories about the fascinating Princess Caraboo began to circulate throughout society, and Mrs Worrall, who – thanks to her princess – had become the most popular hostess in England almost overnight. And so Mrs Worrall took her to **fashionable** Bath, where she held a ball in the princess's honour. Crowds of people came to see her.

Eventually the stories made the newspapers and that, as in the case of so many celebrities, was the cause of Princess

Caraboo's downfall. One day a Mrs Neale, who kept a boarding house in Bristol, opened the *Bristol Journal* and was surprised to read the princess's story. For **she recognised Caraboo** at once – and NOT as a princess but as one of her lodgers, who six months ago had been so down on her luck she had taken to begging to pay the rent. She was clever though, and after a while reckoned she would make more money if she had a story up her sleeve – something outrageous, something colourful, something that would appeal to people's sympathies. So she designed herself an exotic turban and she made up a mysterious language, and for this, passers-by soon rewarded her not with just pennies but with silver coins instead. **Ker-ching!**

Hmm, thought Mrs Neale as she cut out the story from the paper, put it in her bag and set off for Almondsbury. Mrs Neale knocked on the door at Knole Park and asked to see Mrs Worrall. 'Your princess is no princess,' she exclaimed. 'She's a cobbler's daughter from Witheridge, and her name is not Caraboo – it's Mary Willcocks!' Later

— A PERFECTLY PREPOSTEROUS PRINCESS PRANK —

that day Caraboo was due to have another sitting with Mr Bird the portrait painter. So imagine her surprise when she arrived to find her old landlady waiting for her with her hostess, Mrs Worrall, instead.

The fake princess eventually broke down and confessed all. She'd been born into a very poor family, six of her brothers and sisters had died in childhood and she'd

been forced to make her living working on local farms or spinning and weaving wool from the age of eight. Eventually she ended up in the care of a clergyman who found her work with a family called Matthews. The Matthewses thought her eccentric but actually rather engaging. She seemed to be able to charm people of all kinds, including the neighbours' Jewish cook, and it is thought Mary learned to recognise the Hebrew alphabet from her and perhaps a few words too. But for lots of poor people at that time things sometimes went seriously wrong, and so she was confined at St Mary's Workhouse in London and the Magdalen Hospital for women – not a hospital like one of ours, but another sort of prison, really, for women who were thought to be unfit to live in normal society during those horrible times.

When Mrs Worrall heard this tale, she was somewhat conflicted. On the one hand she was angry to have been duped, but on the other she had once been a stranger too and could not help but be moved by

Mary's story. And she had rather enjoyed the excitement Caraboo had brought to Knole Park. Mr Worrall, meanwhile, had been conducting his own research. He had sent off some of the strange writings Caraboo had provided for him in her own 'language' to some scholars at Oxford. When the results came back they concluded **her language was total nonsense**. Also, a doctor recognised the strange marks on her head as the scars left by a medical technique called 'hot cupping', when doctors would heat up little metal cups and apply them to someone's head, back or chest. This created a vacuum so the cups would sort of suck up the flesh they were stuck to so that any 'impurities' in the body would be somehow sucked up too. Needless to say, all it did to their patients – many of them poor inmates of the workhouse – was leave them with scars.

Mr Worrall was furious *again* but once more Mrs Worrall managed to calm him down. Instead of arresting the fake princess, Mrs Worrall arranged for her to leave quietly to find a living and a life somewhere else. But where?

Perhaps Philadelphia? thought Mrs Worrall, in her homeland of America, and so the Worralls paid for her fare and that of a chaperone (someone to accompany her), and she set sail across the Atlantic Ocean. And so, unlike Princess Caraboo, Mary Willcocks really *did* sail the Bristol Channel, only going in the other direction, west, across the wide, wide sea. There were many more adventures on that voyage, according to some of the stories told about her, but most of them we should take with a pinch of salt (maybe a metric tonne of salt). Here is one of them.

En route, Mary Willcocks (aka the fake princess) made the acquaintance of the most famous man in the world, a man who had defeated many kings and emperors, and even the pope, before his epic fall from power.

The story goes that halfway across the Atlantic the ship was blown off course and Mary found herself landing on a beach at the tiny island of St Helena. Nobody really knew anything about St Helena until the arrival of its most famous resident, **the former Emperor Napoleon**, conqueror of half the world, now defeated and exiled somewhere so far away he would never be a threat to anyone ever again. But it just so happened that Mary's ship somehow ended up there, and it also just so happened that Napoleon was taking a walk on the beach that very same day and bumped into her. It is then said that he was so enchanted by the preposterous princess he even wanted to appeal to the pope for permission to marry her. *Did he?* Probably not. St Helena was not exactly on the way from Bristol to Philadelphia and even if it *were* true, would he really have wanted to marry a fake princess who everyone knew was a cobbler's daughter from Witheridge? And would he really have wanted the permission of the pope to marry her when not long before he'd had that same pope arrested and exiled? **Sometimes a story is so fascinating**, we want to believe it more than we want to doubt it, no matter what people say.

So I don't know if Caraboo really did meet Napoleon, but whether it's true or not, it tells us something important;

— A HEIST BEFORE BEDTIME —

she was by now so famous that it did not seem unbelievable that she *might* meet Napoleon. The question was, when she got to America would she discover she was as famous over there?

At first the answer seemed to be 'yes'. Crowds of people greeted her on her arrival, curious to see what the preposterous princess was really like. She was quickly engaged to appear on stage at the Washington Hall in Philadelphia. **Unfortunately, curiosity quickly faded away.** Mary was also, remember, a con woman, and that wasn't something people approved of. She even wrote to Mrs Worrall complaining that audiences came to see her not because they were enchanted by her story but because she was notorious for being fake.

In 1824 Mary returned to England, and for a while she appeared as Princess Caraboo on stage in London's fashionable New Bond Street, where she charged a shilling for entrance. She did the same in Bath and Bristol, but even in the city where it had all begun, interest was insufficient.

A PERFECTLY PREPOSTEROUS PRINCESS PRANK

She lived for a while at Bedminster in Somerset, where she married a man called Richard Baker and they had a daughter. She and her husband became leech-brokers, providing unlovely **bloodsucking creatures** (leeches) to doctors at the Bristol Infirmary (what hospitals used to be called). It was medical practice at the time to stick leeches on to the flesh of patients in the belief they would suck out any poisons, as well as the blood.

Mary lived into her seventies, still leech-broking, until she died on Christmas Eve 1864 after a nasty fall. She is buried in an unmarked grave at the Hebron Road Cemetery in Bristol. Her daughter carried on leech-broking after Mary died, and lived (just) into the twentieth century in a house she shared with many cats.

One day in Bristol on a bank holiday weekend in 2022, a mysterious statue appeared in the Hebron Road Cemetery. The statue shows a seated young woman in an elegant dress, complete with headdress and feathers, holding a mask on a stick in front of her, but not covering her face. We can guess the identity of the subject – it is of course **Princess Caraboo** – but the identity of the sculptor is unknown. He or she goes by the name of 'Getting Up To Stuff'. Who could it possibly be? Some say Banksy, another artist from the same city, famous the world over now though his true identity is a closely kept secret. If anyone does know the truth, then one thing is for sure – they're definitely not telling . . .

The Very Hungry Bear Break-in

Lake Tahoe is a huge deep-water lake in America at the edge of the Sierra Nevada mountains. It is sandwiched between Las Vegas and San Francisco and is famous for its natural beauty, clear water, distant peaks, pine trees, water sports and winter sports. But it's also famous for something else . . . an unusually hairy outbreak of thefts that took place in 2021.

Lake Tahoe is popular not only with tourists but also with wildlife. There you will find bald eagles, mule deer, tiny little chipmunks and, best of all, **bears**. Bears love

Lake Tahoe, and Lake Tahoe loves bears. In fact, the number of bears living there has risen quite sharply recently and scientists now reckon there are about 50,000, though it's hard to keep track exactly. Some of them are **grizzly bears** – the ones we are all scared of – but most of them are black bears, which are a bit smaller than grizzlies, and are omnivores, which means they'll eat almost anything, even though their diet is actually largely vegetarian. You still wouldn't want to get on the wrong side of one though . . .

As you can imagine, 50,000 bears competing for food, even in somewhere as large as Lake Tahoe, means there's not always enough to go round. And bears, being bears, will do whatever they have to do to eat, especially in the weeks before hibernation when they stock up with calories to see them through the winter. On top of this, there have been **more and more wildfires** around those parts in recent years, which can burn down the woods and trees where the bears like to live. This means bears end up moving closer to human communities.

THE VERY HUNGRY BEAR BREAK-IN

Black bears are quite idle as animals go, so they like food to be not only plentiful but also easy to come by. Rather than fishing salmon out of the river or climbing trees to get fruit, they would much prefer it if their food was delivered straight to them. After all, wouldn't you like it if you got up in the morning and someone had just left a pile of your favourite things to eat outside your bedroom door? And one of the most reliable sources of food for a bear is often . . . us.

Oh no, I don't mean to say they eat *us* for dinner; bears, for all their fearsome appearance, are **actually quite scared of humans** and will usually keep their distance if they see you. Unless you're *very* unlucky and they're very hungry, or cornered, or they have cubs. But even then, nine times out of ten they'll run away. What I mean to say is they often rely on the food we bring *with us* to the woods – in our picnic hampers and coolers; food that we barbecue and sweets that we eat have all become a rich source of breakfast, lunch and tea for wild bears, especially the bears of Lake Tahoe.

A HEIST BEFORE BEDTIME

So if you don't clear up properly after a picnic at Lake Tahoe, **once you've gone the bears will turn up** and eat whatever you've left behind. Bears can't go to the supermarket like we can, or light up the barbie to grill a chicken wing, squirt ketchup on a hot dog or cook porridge over a stove. They need us to do that for them, and so they hang around in campsites and picnic areas at Lake Tahoe to hoover up our leftovers.

And that's not all. Once bears have the taste for human food, they'll rummage through rubbish bins too, looking for half a sausage, a banana or a marmalade sandwich, which as we all know is normally the diet of a different kind of bear from a very different part of the Americas. Anyway, as I was saying, the more food the visitors to Lake Tahoe left behind, the more the bears got to eat, and the more they got to eat, the more they wanted to eat and *that* is how one day something quite unexpected happened – a bear called Hank the Tank pulled off one of the **most daring food heists in history!**

It all started during the Covid-19 crisis, back in 2020, when lots of people who had holiday homes on Lake Tahoe decided to sit out lockdown there rather than in the city. It was much nicer to spend the lovely spring weather by the lakeside than stuck indoors. More people spending more time picnicking around the lake meant more free dinners for bears, and because some of those lockdowners did not know much about bear behaviour, they even left food out for them, thinking they were doing them a favour. Well, they *were* doing the bears a favour, but they weren't doing themselves any! **Bears are clever animals** and did not need telling twice where a free dinner could be found. So it wasn't long before the bears started coming round for breakfast, lunch and even tea, whether food was left out for them or not.

I say *they*, but actually there was one bear who kept coming back over and over again, and that bear was ABSOLUTELY ENORMOUS. Now, a black bear would normally weigh around 136 kg (which is about the weight of twenty sausage dogs). But this bear had grown to about 230 kg (which is about the weight of a piano). And if *you'd* have seen Hank *you'd* have said he was enormous too; he was SO huge that people started taking photographs of him and posting them on social media. There, they called him 'Yogi', 'Chunky' and the 'Big Guy', but the name that really stuck was 'Hank the Tank'. **Why had Hank got so big?** Partly because there were so many easy calories to harvest from human leftovers, but also because with so much food around, there was no need for him to hibernate. So Hank just kept eating and eating and got bigger and bigger . . . and bigger.

Hank the Tank was not only big but brainy and bold too – brainy enough to work out where free dinners came from, and bold enough to simply help himself. At first he just turned up outside people's houses. But after a while he got a bit more adventurous and began to go through their bins.

By 2021, Hank had become so bold that he started to

THE VERY HUNGRY BEAR BREAK-IN

invite himself inside people's houses! Bears, as I said, are intelligent creatures and can work out how to lift latches or turn door handles. But Hank was even more enterprising than that, and like his namesake 'Tank', he simply forced his way in.

He **knocked** down garage doors, which crumpled like cardboard; he **barged** through windows, leaving a shower of broken glass; and he **shoved** through front doors, which he would simply swat off their hinges, not even stopping to wipe his paws. Once he even broke through a wall, squeezed into a gap under a house and clawed his way in through the floor! As soon as he was inside, Hank would make his way to the kitchen, larder or fridge, or even upstairs, helping himself to his favourite snacks (bears have a very good sense of smell).

Within a year, twenty-eight houses in the Tahoe Keys (a posh marina on the south of the lake) had reported bear break-ins. On one occasion Hank had even smashed a window and squeezed into a house on Catalina Drive while the people who lived there were actually in! They ran away and called the cops, who rushed over and banged on the outside of the house until Hank ran out of the back door and disappeared into the nearby woods.

The bear-burgled residents of Lake Tahoe wanted something done about it. Why was a giant bear boldly barging in and grabbing their grub? How had Hank the Tank got past the security gates at the bottom of the drive? What were they supposed to do if they came home to find the door off its hinges and a bear burping in the bedroom? And just *what* were the authorities going to do about it? So many people had dialled 911 to report bear break-ins that the police said they couldn't handle any more. So they called in the cavalry, which in this case was the California Department of Fish and Wildlife, whose job it was to deal with bears.

The first thing they did was send a team to Lake Tahoe to give basic bear-management classes to the anxious residents. The team explained what the bears were doing

THE VERY HUNGRY BEAR BREAK-IN

and how best to deal with them – i.e. *not* by shooting them, as some of the frightened householders wanted to do, but by rounding them up and moving them out of harm's way. The department also began some **detective work**. The first thing they discovered was that Hank was not a single bear that had gone rogue; in fact, there were at least three bears who were breaking into people's homes. It was hard to tell one bear from another though, so everyone just blamed Hank. Also, when they tested Hank's DNA (a sort of recipe that scientists can extract from a strand of hair, or a splodge of saliva, or even a bogey for all I know, which tells them exactly who, or what, it came from) they discovered the BIGGEST SURPRISE OF ALL – Hank was not male, but female! **Yes . . . girl power!**

Actually 'mummy power', because Hank had three cubs and was bold not just from greediness (although she certainly wasn't likely to saunter past a free dinner) but also because she needed to feed her cubs. How long would it be before the cubs learned to follow in their mother's pawsteps and become **bear-burglars** themselves?

Meanwhile, the team from the department had started tracking Hank and eventually traced her to a house in Lake Tahoe where she had made a den with her cubs. They fired a special dart into her side that made her fall deeply

THE VERY HUNGRY BEAR BREAK-IN

asleep. They tagged her, and when she woke up they were able to track her movements. And that is how they finally proved that Hank (or Bear 64F as the department were now calling her) was the most successful bear-burglar of all, with at least twenty break-ins to her name. Something had to be done.

On 7 August 2023 they captured Hank and her cubs and, while they slept, put them safely behind bars while the department decided what to do. Now, in most cases when bears get used to being too near humans they are often put to sleep for fear of them becoming too much of a danger, but by now Hank had lots of fans and when they heard the bears might be put down, Hank's fans started a campaign to spare them. 'Don't put Hank and her cubs to sleep!' they said. 'Find them somewhere else to live!' Three wildlife sanctuaries offered to give Hank a new home, and the BEAR League, a charity dedicated to bears, said they would cover the costs of relocating her.

Eventually the department bowed to pressure and Hank

A HEIST BEFORE BEDTIME

was **relocated to a wildlife reserve in Colorado**. She was now a celebrity and was welcomed in by the state governor, who renamed her Henrietta. Henrietta was carefully looked after, checked by vets and eventually given three hundred acres to roam in, planted with her favourite pine trees. Best of all, her food was delivered by rangers, meaning she no longer had to raid fridges.

As for the cubs, they were also relocated, but to a different spot where it was thought they would better adapt to life in the wild instead of living off other people's pizzas. The cubs were driven to a remote part of the Sierra Nevada mountains and sent scampering off into their new lives. They were fitted with tracking collars so the department knew where they were. After about nine months, the collars dropped off so they could be collected and reused.

And so Henrietta and her cubs went on to live their new lives, and the residents of Lake Tahoe got peace of mind and slices of pizza back. Everyone learned an important lesson: do not mess with the natural order of things! Bears are bears and need to live a beary life. Humans are humans and need to live a human life. Mix them together and you might just mess both lives up.

Around Lake Tahoe today there are special bear-proof bins, picnickers make sure they take their leftovers home and *everybody* is careful not to leave out free meals for any . . .

. . . Bears!

The Fake Fairies of Cottingley

During the First World War, more than a hundred years ago now, two cousins called Frances Griffiths and Elsie Wright lived at Cottingley, a village near Bradford in Yorkshire. Frances was nine and had come from South Africa with her mum to live in England with her Aunt Polly, Uncle Arthur and sixteen-year-old cousin, Elsie.

The two girls had **loads of fun** playing by the beck, a little stream that ran through the bottom of their garden. They loved it so much they were constantly getting wet. So one day when Elsie's mum, Polly, got fed up of drying their clothes, she asked them why they had to play there all the time. The girls answered, 'FAIRIES!'

Fairies? Yes, that's right. For the bottom of the garden is where Elsie and Frances met the fairies who came to play there. How would you feel if you had fairies at the bottom of *your* garden? You would want to play there all day too, *right?*

Polly was not persuaded by this story. Of course there weren't any fairies at the bottom of her garden; she would have seen them if there were. But Elsie insisted, saying they only appeared to her and Frances. When her mum was still not persuaded, Elsie said she would prove it. But how? **By taking their picture, of course.**

It just so happened that Elsie's dad, Arthur, was a keen amateur photographer and so he had a camera. Cameras in those days were not like the ones everyone has on their phone today; they were bulky, boxy things made of wood, but, thanks to her dad, Elsie knew just how to use one. So she and Frances went down to the beck with the camera and came back half an hour later with the evidence they needed. They had photographed the fairies.

In 1917 you didn't just take a picture and instantly see the image like you do nowadays; you had to take the glass plate out of the camera in a special darkroom and develop it using chemicals. These chemicals made the image gradually appear like something coming at you through the mist on a winter's morning. But what an image started to emerge as Elsie's father developed their picture! It showed Frances down at the beck, resting her head on her hand with a little garland of flowers in her hair looking intently in front of her and half smiling. This was charming enough, but what she was in front of her was the real star of the photo – for there in the image were **four fairies frolicking in the flora**. They stood about fifteen centimetres tall and were wearing the sort of gossamer outfit you'd expect a fairy to wear, with lovely wings, and one of them playing some sort of pipe. The image is slightly blurred (high-res wasn't a thing back then) and, to be honest, now that we're

used to seeing AI create images that can be impossible to tell apart from real ones, you *might* say they looked a bit – well, clunky. But you have to imagine what it was like at a time when technology was only just emerging (people didn't even have TVs back then!). So to see a photograph of fairies was **mind-blowing**. Polly gasped when she saw it. There really were fairies at the bottom of the garden! Meanwhile Arthur, who knew a bit about photography, thought differently. He felt sure the girls were pulling his leg and had faked the image. He knew Elsie was a good artist and so it was much more likely they were not *real* fairies, but cardboard cutouts.

No one said any more about it for a couple of months, and then one day the girls borrowed Arthur's camera again to produce another photograph. This one showed Elsie in a bonnet sitting by the beck looking down on a sort of gnome with wings. It appeared to be prancing around in front of her. **Polly gasped**, like she did the first time, **but Arthur had had enough**. 'No more fairy photography for you,' he said, and forbade the girls from using his camera again. But by now Polly had seen enough to believe them and so, thanks to her, the story of the fairies eventually began to flutter away . . .

A couple of years later, Polly went into Bradford to hear a lecture by someone from the Theosophical Society. This society was formed in New York in 1875 by Madame Blavatsky, who believed that the world is not just about what science can tell us, but also the supernatural (hidden realms beyond our world that you can't always see), and that you need both to make sense of it. It just so happened that one of the things Madame Blavatsky believed in was . . . fairies. In fact, 'Fairies' was the very topic of the lecture Polly had gone to listen to – how thrilled she must have been to hear it! After the talk, Polly made her way to the lecturer to show him the fairy photographs she had carefully brought from home in her bag. The lecturer was amazed and quickly showed them to other members of the society, who asked if they could borrow them. Polly agreed, so the society sent copies of them around the various branches of their club. That is how they came to be seen by a man called Edward Gardner.

Edward Gardner, president of the London branch of the Theosophical Society, was fascinated by the photos. As the Theosophists believed there was a world beyond this one, it meant that if the photos **were real**, here was the **evidence**.

Gardner sent the photographs to his friend Harold Snelling, who was an expert in photography, to see what he thought of them. Snelling replied that the photographs had not been tampered with and that they reflected what had really been in front of the camera when they were taken. To be fair, he didn't actually say they really *were* fairies, just that the image had not been faked by photographic techniques. But that was good enough for Gardner. He asked Snelling to tidy the images up a bit and make them look a bit sharper. He then asked him to make some prints to take on tour around the country. And so news of the fairies spread its wings.

The story spread so far that it eventually reached a very important person, Sir Arthur Conan Doyle. Conan Doyle was the creator of an extremely famous detective you may have heard of – Sherlock Holmes, **the most brilliant puzzle-cracker who ever cracked a puzzle**. The Sherlock Holmes stories had made Conan Doyle famous, rich and very influential. He was also *very* interested in the paranormal. 'Paranormal' describes events that cannot be explained by science and includes things like ghosts, UFOs and, of course . . . fairies. In fact, Conan Doyle had been commissioned to write an article about fairies for *The Strand Magazine*, so when he heard that someone had actually managed to photograph some and that Gardner had copies of the pictures, he wrote to him immediately and asked to see them.

The famous writer was captivated. Perhaps this is a surprise, for Conan Doyle started out as a medic – a man of science – who believed in evidence and reason (the character of Sherlock Holmes was even based on his old lecturer at Edinburgh Medical School). So why would he of all people think that these really were fairies in the photographs? Well, even scientists occasionally believe what they want to believe rather than what evidence tells them. On top of that there had been a **big surge of interest in the paranormal** during and after the First World War, when so many lost their lives, including

Conan Doyle's own son. Maybe it brought the grieving comfort to think there was a place somewhere beyond this life where those we have lost live still. And if there *is* a place beyond this world then maybe it's a world where fairies live, and *maybe* they can even fly between that world and ours, all the way to Cottingley.

So that's how Conan Doyle wrote to Arthur Wright, asking for his permission to use the photographs in the article he was writing. And Arthur granted it, even though he still thought the photos might have been faked. Maybe Arthur thought he could make a few quid out of them? The photographs *did* go on to generate a lot of money but Arthur Wright didn't benefit from this (Gardner and Conan Doyle did). Or *maybe* it was because he was so impressed that someone as important as Conan Doyle had taken an interest in them? Who knows . . . but Conan Doyle and Gardner sent the pictures off to Kodak, the biggest outfit in the world for making and processing camera films back then. Although Kodak found no evidence of fakery, they didn't say the fairies were real either; nor, for that matter, did Eastman, the other big photographic laboratory of the time. In fact, Eastman thought they *had* been faked, but this was still not enough to change the minds of Gardner and Conan Doyle. Gardner had them made into postcards, which he sold on his lecture tour, and Conan Doyle was cracking on with his article for *The Strand Magazine*.

If you look at this photo today you would see that the fairies look flat, like cutouts; there are no shadows on them, unlike on Elsie and Frances, and, to be honest, the fairies also look like they've just been to an Edwardian hairdresser and dressmaker rather than fluttered out of the fairy realm. Despite this, the pictures still sent the fairies **fluttering around the world**.

There was now so much interest in the fairies that in 1920 Conan Doyle and Gardner gave the girls a camera and asked if they could try to take some more pictures of the fairies. Elsie and Frances agreed, went down to the beck when the weather was favourable (unaccompanied, of course, because the fairies appeared only to them) and returned triumphantly with three more exposures. (Exposures are what in the early 1900s we called photos before they had been developed.) **The images were captivating.** One showed Frances looking beguiled by a fairy dancing right in front of her face, another showed a fairy offering a 'posy of harebells' to Elsie, and a third showed the fairies sunbathing.

The new photos were sent off to Gardner and Conan Doyle, who were delighted with them. Conan Doyle published the photos in his article for *The Strand Magazine* with an account of how Elsie and Frances had taken them, though he changed their names to Iris and Alice Carpenter. The magazine was an instant sell-out, and for a while the fairies and 'the Carpenter girls' were talked about everywhere. **Some loved the fairy pictures and thought they were real.** But many others were unpersuaded. One commentator wrote '... knowing children, and knowing that Sir Arthur Conan Doyle has legs, I decide that the Miss Carpenters have pulled one of them'.

The Miss Carpenters' identity was soon discovered, and the girls became celebrities. Conan Doyle wrote a second article for *The Strand Magazine* and also a book, *The Coming of the Fairies*, which created even more interest. In 1921 Gardner came to visit Cottingley, bringing with him one of the leading occultists of the day, Geoffrey Hodson. An occultist is someone who believes in – and often believes they can see – **supernatural forces** such as magic and fairies. Once there, Hodson actually claimed to see fairies jumping around everywhere! The girls, however, were a bit tired of the fairies by now and all the kerfuffle around them but, nevertheless, when questioned both girls stuck to their story – the fairies were real and they had really photographed them.

Over the years, interest in the Cottingley fairies eventually died down. Frances and Elsie grew up, married, had families and moved abroad. And that probably would have been the end of the story if Elsie had not returned to England.

Nearly fifty years after Elsie took the first photograph, a journalist with a nose for an unfinished story tracked her down and asked her if she *really* had seen and photographed fairies. This time, Elsie replied they *may* have been figments of her imagination but maybe, just *maybe*, figments can flit into photos; maybe the camera can see what we can't? This rekindled the public's curiosity and in 1971 a report about the Cottingley fairies appeared on television. Elsie stuck to her story. She could not explain what they had seen but claimed that neither she nor Frances had made it up. Then in 1976 the two were interviewed on television and again both denied any mischief. However, following this, a team of photography experts reviewed the pictures and finally concluded they *were* faked.

In 1983, nearly a lifetime after the first picture appeared, Elsie and Frances **finally confessed**:

THE FAIRY PHOTOGRAPHS WERE FAKED!

A HEIST BEFORE BEDTIME

And so the real story unravelled. It turned out that when Frances had come to live with Elsie, she'd brought with her from South Africa a book called *Princess Mary's Gift Book*. Inside, it was illustrated with pictures of fairies. Elsie copied them, changed them a bit, coloured them in and then cut them out. The girls then fixed the cutouts on hatpins, stuck them in the ground and posed with them for the camera. Finally they chucked the fairies in the beck so no one would find them.

At first it was just a prank to tease Arthur and Polly for doubting their story about the fairies at the bottom of

the garden. Elsie had worked at a photographic studio in Bradford where they used a technique to show soldiers who had been lost in the war looking like they had come home to their families, some comfort for grieving mothers, fathers, brothers and sisters. Because of this, she knew a bit about how a photograph can tell a gentler story when the reality is too hard to bear. She was also aware that a photo can give you a reason to believe in something you desperately want to believe in. What she did *not* foresee was how those pictures would fly like fairies away from Cottingley and out into the world. She could not have predicted that suddenly **Sir Arthur Conan Doyle** himself would be involved, as well as newspapers and magazines. It all just seemed easier to say nothing at all than to make so many people suddenly **look like fools**. Well, *maybe* that's the reason. I think Elsie had a bit of mischief in her too, otherwise why not say they couldn't find any fairies when Gardner came up to Cottingley and they were asked to take some more pictures of them?

For Frances it was perhaps a little different. I think she really *did* believe in fairies – she always insisted she could see them, even though the photographs were faked. Frances maintained to her dying day that the last of the photographs, the photo of the fairies sunbathing by the beck, was in fact real (even though Elsie denied it).

To this very day, the story of the fairies still continues to flutter. We're talking about them now, aren't we? There have been books written about them, films made about them and there are *still* people who insist that they too can see fairies – **fairies that live at the bottom of their garden**.

The Burglar and the Bugle

It is always worth pausing before we give a round of applause to a robber. Not all of them are like Robin Hood, who stole from the rich to give to the poor. Some robbers just take stuff simply for the glory of taking it. And this is how our story begins . . .

Stéphane Breitwieser was born in 1971 in Mulhouse, France, a colourful city near the border with Germany. The Schlumpf Collection can be found at Mulhouse, which is the largest collection of cars in the world, famous above all for its 123 Bugattis, including Signor Bugatti's very own Coupé Napoléon, which he crashed when he dozed off at the wheel in 1931 (it was fixed before it went on display). The car is so precious that during the Second World War Bugatti had it bricked up in a secret chamber to keep the Nazis from taking it. So all this is to say that Stéphane grew up in a place where they knew about precious things. Precious things cost money though, and Stéphane, who lived with his mum, Mireille, did not have the resources to buy them himself. **So he decided to steal them instead.**

As far as we can tell, Stéphane started stealing treasures at the age of twenty-three when on a visit to the French town of Thann. There, he pinched an old flintlock pistol from its museum. A year later he stole a crossbow from another museum in Alsace. You might think he was starting a collection of antique weapons, but not according to his next theft . . . which took place on a visit to Gruyères in Switzerland. Gruyères is where the famous Gruyère cheese comes from – you know, the cheese with the holes in? Well,

Stéphane was not after some cheese, but he *was* interested in the holes in security at the city's castle.

On a visit there his eyes were drawn to a little painting of a young woman, which he thought was painted by the great Dutch master Rembrandt. Only it wasn't. It was actually painted by Christian Wilhelm Ernst Dietrich, a much less famous painter who was working a hundred years later in the 1740s. Dietrich's speciality was painting in the style of others, and one of the painters he was best at copying was Rembrandt.

Stéphane was visiting the museum with his then girlfriend, Anne-Catherine Kleinklaus, and seeing an opportunity (Stéphane was VERY good at seeing opportunities) when the gallery was empty, he asked Anne-Catherine to keep watch. Then he took the painting down, carefully loosened the nails that held the canvas to the frame, pulled them out, rolled up the picture and **hid it in his coat**. And with that Stéphane and Anne-Catherine simply walked out of the museum.

It had been incredibly easy to steal the painting; so easy, in fact, that Stéphane used pretty much the same system for the next six years. He always chose small museums in out-of-the-way places where **security was basic**. Then he would case the joint, looking for cameras and guards. Finally he would return with Anne-Catherine, who would create a diversion. Then, while the attention was focused on her, Stéphane would simply take the picture off the wall, or, if it were fixed or there were sensors, he'd cut the canvas out of the frame with his Swiss Army Knife. It worked so well that between 1995 and 2001 Stéphane Breitwieser stole a grand total of **239 artworks** from **172 museums** – and those are just the ones we know about.

Stealing all those treasures must have made him rich, right? But in fact Stéphane wasn't rich at all. He worked as a waiter, and not even the best waiter with the best tips in the world would earn enough to buy even the least valuable of the things he stole. However, unlike most art thieves, Stéphane didn't do it for the money. **He did it**

because he loved art and he loved it *so* much that he wanted to own it rather than just visit it in a gallery or a museum. Do *you* have a favourite painting or treasure in a museum or gallery? I do; it's a giant white pot from Korea made in the 1700s. It is displayed now in the British Museum and it's called a 'moon jar' because it looks as big and round and pale as the moon. I have loved it for years and years. Whenever I have a spare afternoon in London, I call in to see it. I wouldn't mind having it at home, but I don't want to steal it and even if I tried (and I wouldn't), I'd need a tent to smuggle it out, so I don't think I would get very far. Also, I like the idea of other people enjoying it just as much as I do. But back to Stéphane . . .

Stéphane's desire to take home the things he loved was so **intense** that before long his bedroom was stuffed with the treasures he stole. He closed the curtains to protect them from too much light, and there, he and Anne-Catherine had them all to themselves. Nobody else got to see them apart from a picture framer who reframed them for Stéphane (but he didn't know what they were) and his mum (but she thought they'd been picked up in flea markets and junk shops).

It's extraordinary – *239 works of art*! As well as the pistol and the crossbow and the Rembrandt (that wasn't a Rembrandt), Stéphane stole paintings by Brueghel, Watteau and Teniers, who are all world famous. He also stole porcelain and ivories and sculptures and buckles and

musical instruments, and, all combined, they were worth an **amazing £750m**.

SEVEN HUNDRED AND FIFTY MILLION POUNDS! HANGING ON THE WALL OF A BEDROOM IN MULHOUSE! Stéphane may not have been much interested in money, but he still described himself as one of the wealthiest men in Europe.

The most valuable item Stéphane ever stole was a painting by Lucas Cranach the Elder, a portrait of the Electoral Princess Sibylle of Saxony, which is *quite* the mouthful. It was painted in the 1500s and was on display for an auction at a castle in Baden-Baden, Germany. Stéphane went to take a look, and when no one was watching he carried out his usual trick – he cut the painting out of the frame, hid it in his jacket and walked out of the castle. The painting in today's money was worth about £9m.

Imagine that? Walking out of somewhere with £9m stuffed up your jumper? No wonder Stéphane found that once he started stealing stuff, **he just couldn't stop.**

Until he *had* to stop, that is. It all began going wrong in 1997 when Stéphane and Anne-Catherine tried to pinch a painting by the Dutch master Willem van Aelst, remembered mostly for his gorgeous paintings of flowers, fruit and game. *This* painting was of a landscape belonging to a Swiss collector who had his own private gallery. Stéphane arranged to visit the gallery. Then, while the owner was distracted, he helped himself to the painting and he and Anne-Catherine made off with it like they usually did. But THIS time the owner twigged what was happening and came running after them! 'STOP, THIEF!' he called. And he caught them just as they were getting into Stéphane's mum's car.

The police were called and found not only the van Aelst **but another stolen picture in the boot of the car too**. 'You're nicked!' they said, only it was in Switzerland where, confusingly, they speak four languages so it could have been in French – 'Je vous arrête!' or German – 'Du wirst festgenommen!' or Italian – 'È arrestatu!' or it could have been Romansh – 'Vus èl'arrestau!'

THE BURGLAR AND THE BUGLE

Whatever the language, it meant the same thing. Stéphane was finally brought before a judge and found guilty of theft. It was his first offence in Switzerland, so the sentence, luckily for him, was light. He got eight months in jail, but it was a suspended sentence, so he wasn't actually locked up. He was also banned from entering Switzerland for three years.

They should have locked him up, really, because with barely a pause to catch his breath he returned to Switzerland, this time travelling under his mother's maiden name, and continued his one-man (plus girlfriend) **crime spree**. He was so confident – cocky even – that he returned to galleries that he had *already* pinched art from in the past and stole some more! Over the next three years Stéphane simply *stuffed* his darkened bedroom with more and more . . . and more **stolen art**. It must have looked like Tutankhamun's tomb in there when Howard Carter opened it up thousands of years after it was sealed and exclaimed, 'I SEE SUCH TREASURES!'

But then it went *properly* wrong. And it was all because of a bugle. A bugle – in case you're wondering – is a brass instrument that looks a bit like a trumpet, only smaller, and is often used by the military (it's also a type of minty plant but that is *not* what Stéphane stole).

In the November of 2001, on a trip to Switzerland, Stéphane visited the Richard Wagner Museum near Lucerne. It was there in the 1860s that Wagner, **one of the greatest opera composers of his time** – of any time, really – lived at the Villa Tribschen. Wagner, like Stéphane, was a bit of a magpie, and crammed the house with paintings, sculptures, furniture, textiles and artefacts, including the death mask of his former friend and famous philosopher, Friedrich Nietszche. **He also owned a bugle**. What it was doing there I don't know because I'm pretty sure Wagner doesn't use a bugle in any of his operas (he does use hunting horns, and special tubas as well as a complete set of tuned anvils, but I'm pretty sure there are no bugles). Anyway, one day Stéphane visited

THE BURGLAR AND THE BUGLE

the villa – this time on his own – and he took the bugle, which was hung on a silken cord, and brought it home. This caused a great big row with Anne-Catherine, who was beginning to think their life of crime was going nowhere; she was furious that he had risked pinching something in Switzerland of all places, the one country where his crimes were known about and where the police had sets of both their fingerprints. She insisted on accompanying Stéphane back to the scene of the crime to make sure everything was wiped down properly. Stéphane agreed, so they returned to the Villa Tribschen.

Anne-Catherine went in alone while Stéphane went for a stroll outside, but unfortunately he was spotted lurking in the car park by a man walking a dog. It just so happened that the dog walker had seen a report in the paper about the theft and so a lurking man naturally raised his suspicions. He quickly reported Stéphane to the woman on reception, who took one look at him and recognised him immediately. **The police were called.**

A HEIST BEFORE BEDTIME

They arrived, and Stéphane was arrested and taken to the station to be interrogated. There, he denied everything – who he was, what he was doing and any knowledge of a bugle. This wasn't enough to convince the police though, so they put him in a cell and there he stayed for a surprisingly long time. Days turned into weeks. Why was he still being detained? Because the police knew about the theft of the van Aelst painting from the private collector and had been sorting out a warrant to search Stéphane's flat, *that's* why.

So Stéphane spent a miserable Christmas and New Year in the cells. Finally he was interrogated again. Only *this* time the police had a big pile of photographs. They took one out and laid it on the table in front of him. 'Do you recognise this?' they asked. He did. It was of a medal he'd stolen from a different museum in Switzerland. They produced another photograph, and another and another and another, and then eventually **one of the very first things Stéphane had ever stolen**, the flintlock pistol from the museum at Thann seven years before.

THE BURGLAR AND THE BUGLE

There was nothing for it but to confess. Stéphane told the police what they wanted to know, identifying each object from the photograph. It was a long interview, but it could have been much longer if they'd had photographs of ALL the artworks Stéphane had stolen in his seven-year career as a thief. There were more than 300, from the £9m portrait of the princess to an ostrich egg that had been mounted in silver and turned into a special drinking cup. Stéphane couldn't help but notice from the photographs that his stolen treasures did not *exactly* look in brilliant condition – certainly not as he would have kept them. It was only when he saw the label on the front of the dossier of photographs that he realised why the treasures looked in such poor condition. The label said they had been **recovered from the Rhone-Rhine Canal**, a waterway that meanders not very far from where he lived. How had these objects that he loved so much ended up in the canal, like any old shopping trolley?

And then another question came to him. Why had the

police not produced any photographs of the *paintings* he had stolen? I wonder if at that moment Stéphane's blood really did run cold, not because he was looking at some serious jail time, but because he realised what had happened to his precious hoard of lovely things.

This is what had happened . . .

As soon as Anne-Catherine got back to Mulhouse she told Stéphane's mum he'd been arrested and then the whole story came out. Stéphane's mum went into shock. **Three hundred stolen artworks stashed in her son's bedroom?** Her son who was at that very moment being interrogated by the Swiss police? The police could get a warrant to search her flat where half a museum's worth of stolen artwork was hidden right now? *Uh-oh.*

In a panic Stéphane's mum quickly decided the only thing to do was dispose of the evidence. She filled bags with sculptures and antique pistols and special ostrich eggs and whatever else she could manage, and made trip after trip to the canal. When she was sure no one was looking, she chucked them all in. And there they lay in the gloop until the police located and recovered them. They looked pretty mucky, but with a bit of luck and some careful conservation *those* treasures were eventually restored and put back on display in the places they'd been taken from.

But what of the pictures, like the £9m portrait? Well, I'm sorry to say that Stéphane's mum destroyed them. Some she cut up and put down the garbage disposal. Others, like

the ones that were painted on panels of wood, she took to the forest nearby, built a bonfire, then tossed them into the flames. **Priceless picture after priceless picture went up in smoke.** And when the police finally got a warrant to search the flat all they found was the silken cord the bugle had hung from. Stéphane's mum and Anne-Catherine were both arrested.

Imagine what a blow that must have been for Stéphane when he found out. Not only were his mum and his girlfriend in custody, but **far, far worse** for him – *I* think – was the discovery that his precious pictures had been burned to ashes and were lost to the world forever!

Eventually all three confessed and in 2005 the Swiss courts found all three guilty. Stéphane's mum got three years in jail for destroying other people's property, Anne-Catherine got eighteen months for receiving stolen items and Stéphane got three years for the many, many thefts. Crime does not pay; the world's greatest art thief had ended up in the slammer, and not only did he lose the very things he coveted the most but because of his thievery they had been destroyed and **lost forever**. What a torment it must be for him to think of that bonfire in the woods! He'd *surely* learned his lesson, hadn't he?

Nope. After he was released, more stolen artworks ended up in his possession and in 2013 Stéphane served another prison sentence. Then after that in 2023 the police discovered stolen Roman coins at Stéphane's flat. When they searched his mother's place they found €163,000 concealed in buckets. This time Stéphane was sentenced to house arrest and had to wear a tag around his ankle.

Eventually Stéphane wrote a book about his life of crime, called *Confessions d'un voleur d'art* (which translates as *Confessions of an Art Thief*), and his story has been told in dozens of papers, magazines, online sites and even in books written by others. Perhaps his fame is some recompense. I don't know. But I *do* know that by becoming so famous he became **instantly recognisable too**, so if he so much as pokes his nose round the door of a museum or gallery the security guards would be on him like a rugby scrum. Perhaps *that* is his biggest punishment . . .

And as for the dog walker who dobbed him in? The museum was so grateful to him for the tip-off they rewarded him with a lifetime supply of dog food.

A Deadly Dangerous Bug Caper

I was once a contestant on *I'm A Celebrity Get Me Out Of Here* – a great gig for anyone who loves insects because I can't think of a better opportunity anywhere in the world to get up close to spiders and cockroaches, beetles and mealworms, scorpions and maggots, and flies – really weird green ones with long legs and wobbly antennae that hang around in trees and **plop on to your face while you're asleep**. As it happens, I'm *not* someone who loves insects. While I have nothing against them, I'd just rather they stuck to their world and me to mine. But I *was* in their world, so I *had* to get used to them. I'm happy to say we ended up getting on just fine apart from the ones I had to eat in bushtucker trials, but let's not go there because you might have just had your tea and I want you hang on to it.

Anyway, I *say* I can't think of anywhere better to find gobsmackingly interesting insects, but maybe there is *one* place that is – or was – just as good: the Philadelphia Insectarium and Butterfly Pavilion. This incredible insect house was the United States' first **'bug zoo'** when it opened its doors in 1992. Except by 2023 it had closed, so you've missed it.

Were it still open though, and you *could* still visit it, you would be able to feast your eyes on all sorts of brilliant bugs, from tarantulas, praying mantises and ants, to beetles, bees, cockroaches, spiders and scorpions, as well as loads of butterflies, to name just a few of its delights. All the incredible insects that lived there were kept in specially designed displays – some inside and some outside. Flies and

beetles were kept in special tanks alongside animals that rely on insects to live, like lizards and hedgehogs. Going there was a bit like visiting a sort of insect theme park where you could get up close and handle the insects – with the help of specially trained staff, of course. Maybe NOT the

six-eyed sand spider though, known to its friends as *Hexophthalma hahni*, which usually likes to hang around in piles of sand in southern Africa. It wasn't the scariest-looking spider in the insectarium, but you wouldn't want to be bitten by it because it is very poisonous; the poison can **make your flesh start eating itself** and there is no reliable antidote. Someone actually had to have their arm chopped off after they were bitten by one in the wild.

The six-eyed sand spiders and their less frightening friends were looked after by an entomologist in charge, as well as the owner, Steve Kanya, who had founded the insectarium. An entomologist is someone who studies insects. Steve Kanya was an insect expert too but made his living as an exterminator; that's not a baddie from a superhero movie – it's someone who gets rid of infestations of cockroaches and other bugs from places you don't want them to be. Mr Kanya was more interested in insects than in the places people did not want them to be though, so he learned all he could about them. He found a building in the city's north-eastern district, raised some money to buy it and had it converted so it could house **thousands and thousands of creepy-crawlies**. He then hired staff to look after the insects and show them off to visitors. A huge mural of giant orange butterflies flitting across a blue sky was painted on the side of the building, and Mr Kanya's insectarium was ready to open.

Why start an insectarium? Well, if it is butterflies we're talking about the answer is obvious. Who doesn't love butterflies? And visiting the butterfly house at an insectarium is a brilliant way of seeing loads all at once. They flit and flutter and fly and flap; some will even come and perch on your hand, and they come in all different sizes and shapes and colours. There are so many butterflies in a butterfly house it's like being pleasantly attacked by a squadron of fairies. That's worth ten quid and a fight for a parking space, wouldn't you say?

But butterflies are also kept in butterfly houses, insectariums or zoos so entomologists can study them in a convenient location rather than having to climb mountains or cut paths through jungles to find them. And entomologists are interested in all sorts of insects, not just butterflies. They are even interested in the ones that look to us like the really *boring* insects – although nothing is boring, really; you just need to find out what's interesting about it. There were lots of interesting insects in this particular insectarium, one of the most popular being a very nice **Chilean rose hair tarantula** called Aragog, who liked to have his leg hairs stroked.

Anyway, Mr Kanya's Philadelphia Insectarium and Butterfly Pavilion was now officially open. At first things went very well. People liked the insectarium and especially the staff, who were very good at helping schoolkids handle tarantulas and other animals. But what the visitors did not know was that was behind the scenes there was a bit of a battle going on between Mr Kanya and the entomologist. Eventually the entomologist won and took control of the insectarium.

A DEADLY DANGEROUS BUG CAPER

But soon things started to go wrong at the Insectarium. Staff complained that there wasn't enough funding or specific instructions on how to look after the insects properly. Animals need specially trained people to look after them but one member of staff in charge of animal care was not a scientist with loads of experience it was claimed but had only worked for a bit in a pet shop.

The entomologist later denied that any of this was true and the Philadelphia insectarium remained popular with visitors. Then in 2018 something happened that changed everything . . . something that was not only the talk of all Philadelphia, but made the national news as well. What happened? **The most high-profile bug heist in head-scratching history happened, that's what!**

It was just another normal day in the summer of 2018 when the entomologist arrived to open up the museum, but instead of the snores of sleeping grasshoppers (actually, grasshoppers don't snore but they do make a noise that

— A HEIST BEFORE BEDTIME —

sounds like snoring by rubbing their back legs together, but let's not worry about that just now) he heard . . . not a single sound. No snoring . . . no chirping . . . no spidery scampering . . . no fluttering . . . no flapping . . . no flitting . . . no NOTHING.

It turned out that SEVEN THOUSAND insects were missing. That was nearly all of them! Someone had removed 7,000 bugs, from butterflies, scorpions, tarantulas, rhinoceros cockroaches and tiger hissers, to leopard geckos, bumblebee millipedes, African mantises, warty glowspot roaches and EVEN the **six-eyed sand spiders** – and you absolutely, definitely wouldn't want to lose those!

That's $50,000 worth of insects gone in a puff of bug smoke. And, weirder still, not a door had been forced open, a window smashed or an alarm triggered.

There had never been a heist like it. Yes, there have been insect thieves before, but those thieves stole the odd rare specimen. No one had ever before emptied an entire insectarium and stolen 7,000 creepy-crawlies in the night! And when you think about it, how would you actually *catch* 7,000 insects? Turn up with dozens of butterfly nets, open the cases and chase them round the room until you'd got them all? And then what? You could hardly take them home on the bus. You would need a getaway car, and can you imagine jumping into a car or a van holding butterfly nets writhing with burgled bugs, lifted lepidopterae and nicked gnats without causing any kind of commotion? *Ha*, thought the entomologist. *I'll simply check the CCTV footage and find out who did this!* But when he started watching the events from the night before, the entomologist made a **shocking discovery**.

The alleged thieves were his own staff! *That's* why there were no signs of anyone having forced their way in. It was an inside job!

Or – hang on a minute . . . Was it? The investigation began and it wasn't long before a different kind of story unravelled . . .

A HEIST BEFORE BEDTIME

The entomologist called the police, who asked him to identify the culprits from the CCTV footage. This wasn't very difficult because they were his own employees. But wait a second. The police must have thought: if you were going to steal insects from the insectarium you worked in and you *knew* there was CCTV, wouldn't you at least try to disguise yourself? A false moustache, a balaclava, maybe a bee costume?

'Good point,' the staff said when the police came to interview them and they explained that they had not

needed to disguise themselves because they hadn't done anything wrong. They hadn't *stolen* the insects at all because the insects belonged to them and you can't steal something you already own.

So the plot thickened . . .

The staff said that they were so frustrated at trying to run the insectarium without being given what they needed to do the job properly, and they were so fed up with trying to put on a good show while caring for insects without the right support that they had started to bring in their own insects and animals from home. You see, you have to keep replenishing your insectarium when the insects die, whether from not being looked after properly or from old age (they don't live that long – ordinary ants live for just a few weeks and spiders for a couple of years, though a tarantula can make twenty). And when staff left they quite naturally collected their property and took it home with them: their pencil case, the photo of their mum; their pot plant, their **Hotwheels sisyphus** (that really is a type of spider, but I can't be sure they had one at the insectarium; I just thought you might like the name). So this really confused things: *which* insects belonged to the staff, and *which* insects belonged to the entomologist?

When the police put this to the entomologist, he said his staff were all talking rubbish and they were *his* insects, not theirs. So a list was made of what had gone. It turned out that some of the bugs definitely *did* belong to the insectarium, like the **Mexican fireleg tarantula** as well as half a dozen other tarantulas the museum was looking after. The fireleg was quickly found at the home of one of the staff members and brought back. 'See?' said the entomologist. 'They *have* stolen my best insects and they are probably planning to sell them on to other collectors!'

But the police were not sure what to do. By now the newspapers had heard about the theft (that maybe wasn't a theft or maybe *was* a theft) and journalists started asking around. They discovered this was not the first time the entomologist's insectarium had received complaints.

Trisha Nichols, who was put in charge of animal care at the insectarium, claimed that she arrived to find **the place in chaos**, with staff completely fed up. She left and a new director took over, who was the one who started bringing in his own insects and animals and encouraged others to do so too (seeing as so many insects had died).

The staff had also been doing lots of events around Philadelphia, which involved loading up their own cars with insects and animals and showing them to the public, again paying for it themselves, though the entomologist said he had paid everyone back.

After the director was fired, lots of the other members of staff walked out too, claiming they had taken with them the animals they had brought into the insectarium. The staff told the police that the entomologist had seen them do this but he said he had not.

So the police had a good think about it all and decided not to press charges against any of the employees. However, that was not the end of the matter. A TV documentary was made called *Bug Out*, in which some of the former staff members gave their side of the story. The entomologist and Mr Kanya (remember Mr Kanya? The guy who started it but left?) gave their sides of the story too. But after it aired, the entomologist sued the film-makers and former staff members, saying what they claimed happened wasn't the truth and it was damaging to the insectarium's and the entomologist's reputation (the complaint was settled in 2024 and the documentary was removed from all the websites showing it). Because even after everything that happened, the insectarium was still going!

Finally in May 2023, after defaulting on the mortgage payments, it was game over for the insectarium, for the butterflies, scorpions, tarantulas, rhinoceros cockroaches, tiger hissers, leopard geckos, bumblebee millipedes, African mantises, warty glowspot roaches, six-eyed sand spiders and a very nice Chilean rose hair tarantula called Aragog who liked to have his leg hairs stroked. Those that had been returned after the so called 'heist' were found new homes at a conservation organisation called Wild Things Preserve, but it was not open to the public, so the insects' showbiz days were over. **A big party was held for staff and former staff a couple of days before, and then the doors closed for the last time.**

So that was the end of the Philadelphia insectarium; a shame because lots of people like bugs and would love to spend a day out discovering them. Maybe you're one of them? **Well, don't worry, because you can!**

There are some great insectariums still going today that you can try out instead. The oldest insectarium I can think of is at the Artis Royal Zoo in Amsterdam in the Netherlands, which dates back to 1897. It is housed in an old food warehouse – don't worry, they took all the food out first – and if you go you can be shown round by a character called Mijnheer Prikkebeen (I think that's Mr Spindleshanks in English) and walk through a tunnel of grasshoppers if you feel like it.

That's the oldest one, but the biggest one, or at least the

biggest one in North America, is in Montreal in Canada and was opened nearly a hundred years later in 1990. There, you can see ghost mantises, blue scorpions and leaf-cutting ants, many of them donated by a keen entomologist called Brother Firmin, a member of the religious organisation the Christian Brothers, who spent **sixty years collecting more than 100,000 insects**.

Just don't make the mistake of going all the way to Philadelphia to rub the legs of a Chilean rose hair tarantula who possibly still lives there somewhere. If you *do* end up in Philadelphia, don't worry, you can go to see a giant bronze statue of the boxer Rocky Balboa from the Rocky movies instead. But to be honest, it isn't a patch on a Chilean rose hair tarantula.

The Million Dollar McDonald's Heist

Did you know that I am so old that I actually remember visiting the first ever McDonald's in central London not long after it opened? I was sixteen and on a class trip when we stopped at the Charing Cross Station branch, which looked pretty much like a McDonald's today, though it was nearly fifty years ago. It was 1978, the year of the first woman newsreader on ITV, the year the famous cricketer Ian Botham scored a century and took eight wickets on a single innings, and the year 200,000 people came to see the legendary musician Bob Dylan at Blackbushe Aerodrome

(And guess what? I was one of *those* too.)

I had a hamburger and fries, which was quite a thrill because we didn't see hamburgers much in those days. *No cutlery?* I thought when my hamburger arrived, and *Do you call those chips?* when my fries arrived, but we were all very excited to be chomping on our first Maccy D, and probably squirted tomato ketchup all over ourselves and were told off.

Years later I was in Moscow in Russia on the night the first McDonald's opened there – it was a really big deal in 1991, which was also the year the internet started to be available globally, making the World Wide Web possible; the year of the first British woman in space; and the end of the Soviet Union and the beginning of a new era for Russia. **That was why McDonald's was opening up in Moscow** – it couldn't have come to pass without that happening first. It was truly a moment when history changed, symbolised by the queues going round the block and back again of Russians (and me!) trying to get their hands on their first Big Mac.

I'm going on a bit about this partly because, as you will know if you're reading this book, I tend to go on a bit about all sorts of things, but really because McDonald's is not only about burgers and fries and nuggets and the clown with the red hair who looks like he's just walked in from a scary film. It's a massively huge giant of a corporation, with more than **40,000 restaurants** all over the world, selling **6 million burgers** every day. In fact, they've sold so many burgers they stopped counting after the **100 billionth** thirty years ago.

How do you get to be so big? By giving people what they want at a price they can afford. But customers also have to know what's on offer, which means loads of adverts, giveaways and special promotions, and it was a special promotion that led to one of the most outrageous heists in the history of hamburgers.

It all started back in the late 1980s when McDonald's ran a special promotion based on the game of Monopoly. Perhaps you know Monopoly? It's a board game that has been going for ages and ages, and if *you* haven't played it, your mum and dad and grandad and grandma almost certainly have. You throw the dice and move your pieces around a board to buy properties with Monopoly money. Sometimes you have to pay charges or rent for hotels and sometimes you get sent to jail, but the general idea is to end up with all the properties and all the money. Try it some time, it's good fun.

Anyway, McDonald's decided to make stickers with some of these properties on them and put them on the side of cups they sold drinks in. You had to peel them off, see what the property was, and if you got the right combination of properties you could win a prize. The stickers were stuck on the boxes the food came in too, and they even put vouchers on McDonald's adverts in papers and magazines. If you were lucky enough to get a winning combination, most often that would mean free fries, or a McFree McFlurry, but if you were super lucky you could win A MILLION DOLLARS! Imagine that? **Your mum takes you to**

THE MILLION DOLLAR MCDONALD'S HEIST

Maccy D's for a milkshake and you come out with a million dollars?! No wonder everyone loved it and bought burger after burger and shake after shake to see if they could find the winning stickers.

And they *did* win – there were loads of free fries fried, hash browns handed over, McDoubles doled out, and once in a while the big prizes were won too. All over America (because this is where this particular heist happened) people ran out of the restaurants shouting, 'I'VE WON A HOUSE! I'VE WON A CAR! I'M A MILLIONAIRE!'

Only they didn't actually run around all over America – because most of them lived within 25 miles of Lawrenceville, Georgia, home of Jerome Jacobson. Jerome was a former cop working as head of security for the company that took care of the Monopoly campaign for McDonald's. He was such a nice, friendly, trustworthy man that he was known by all as Uncle Jerry. Well, it just so happened Uncle Jerry was responsible for handling all the winning tokens, a job that was *supposed* to ensure they went out across the whole of the country, so everyone got an equal chance of winning. There was just one problem . . .

They didn't! Because Uncle Jerry realised he could send them straight into the hands of his friends and family for a cut of the money instead. This is how it all happened . . .

The winning stickers were kept in a vault at the firm where Uncle Jerry worked. Uncle Jerry would meet up with an independent auditor (someone responsible for making sure everything was done properly so no one could cheat) and together they would take the stickers in a specially sealed briefcase to the McDonald's packaging centres where they were then attached to cups and boxes – selected randomly by a computer. That should have all gone according to plan, but one day the seals that fastened the briefcase (so they could be sure no one got in and messed around with the stickers inside) were mistakenly sent to Uncle Jerry. This meant he now had a way of opening the briefcase after it had been sealed and then resealing it without anyone realising it had been tampered with. Now, when Uncle Jerry and the auditor, who was a woman, arrived at the airport on their way to the packaging centre where they would affix the super-lucky stickers, Uncle Jerry would say he needed to visit the loo, so off he went to the gents' where she couldn't follow. There in a cubicle he would open the briefcase, exchange the winning tokens for ordinary ones, reseal the case, and the auditor would be none the wiser. **Uncle Jerry was in possession of the winning tickets** and he could do what he wanted with them.

A HEIST BEFORE BEDTIME

At first the heist was on the modest side, at least by the standard of some of the other heisters in this book. Uncle Jerry confided in his brother-in-law, passing on to him a stolen $25,000 winning sticker and trusting him not to blab about it to anyone. His brother-in-law cashed in the ticket and shared some of the winnings with Uncle J. His scam had worked, so he did the same for some other trusted family and friends, including his butcher, who got a $200,000 sticker for which he paid Uncle Jerry $45,000.

This carried on and **Uncle Jerry got away with it again and again and again for a year, and then another year, and then another one too.** Soon he had an entire network of people buying winning stickers from him and selling them on for a cut of the money. Actually most of them were pretty random – among them were members of his classic-car club; a man he met in the airport at Atlanta; a psychic; and a Mr Gennaro Colombo, who was a rather dodgy individual in Florida alleged to have gangster connections. His 'customers' like

Mr Colombo passed on the winning tokens to his criminal pals and in return Uncle Jerry took a cut of the winnings. Now, you might think as Uncle J and his gang sold more tickets, and got greedier, it would be easy to make mistakes, or trust the wrong person, meaning the scam would be revealed. But Uncle Jerry was not daft; he insisted that the winning pieces should be passed on to people in other states. This way it would look like the winners were distributed randomly around the country (just like they were supposed to be) and not just in places where Uncle Jerry lived and worked. He also coached them on what to say when they presented their winning tokens at the restaurant so that nothing sounded suspicious.

One day when McDonald's upped the top prize to a million dollars, Uncle Jerry upped his heist too. He stole two of the million-dollar prize-winning tokens, giving one anonymously to a children's hospital – unusually decent behaviour for a fraudster (although it was later said he did this in order to make a judge and jury look more kindly on him if

A HEIST BEFORE BEDTIME

he ever got nicked). The other went to a woman called Gloria, a single mum with very little money. Gloria was friends with the wife of the dodgy guy in Florida I mentioned earlier. His wife had noticed her husband kept selling the stolen stickers to all his buddies, which might arouse suspicion. So she thought of Gloria instead, an African-American woman and not typical at all of her husband's friends' 'customers'. She thought Gloria could use the money so she got her husband to sell her **a million-dollar ticket for $50,000**. But Gloria didn't have $50,000. In order to pay for the ticket, she remortgaged her house then handed the cash over to a dodgy individual by the side of the road (life lesson: if you ever enter into an agreement with someone who requires you to hand over a large amount of money in cash by the side of the road you will probably later regret it). The guy on the road told her what to say when she presented the winning sticker, which was that she was from South Carolina and had found the sticker in her car – this way it could not be traced to a particular restaurant.

So that's what Gloria did. **And it worked**. No one doubted the story and Gloria got the money – a life-changing one million dollars. But it wasn't just the money that changed her life. She'd made a deal with a dodgy individual and he came back to her and demanded more money, then more money, and then more money still. And Gloria felt she had to hand it over or he would drop her in it. It wasn't long before she was in a hopeless mess and wishing she had never got into any of this in the first place. Here's another useful life lesson: easy money most often turns out to be NOT so easy after all. **Also, the chances of someone dropping you in it are quite high.**

And that's exactly what happened. In 2001 an anonymous caller contacted the FBI and told them about a McDonald's Monopoly winner called William Fisher from Jacksonville, Florida who had claimed a $1m prize in 1996 – only *not* in Florida. He had claimed his winnings in New Hampshire, a state 1,500 miles away! That was a bit suspicious, wasn't it? The FBI started looking into it and discovered that actually *many* of the lucky winners could be traced back to Florida rather than to the states where they had claimed their prizes. And, in fact, a suspiciously high number of residents had won Monopoly prizes in Jacksonville, including one family who had won *three* $1m prizes AND a Dodge Viper, a car so cool it once had its own TV series. The FBI started to make more inquiries and it wasn't long before they were led to Uncle Jerry. And they realised the jolly ex-cop from Lawrenceville was actually the mastermind of a heist that had deprived McDonald's customers of tens of millions of dollars in prizes. But it is one thing to suspect someone of a crime and another to convict them in court. And so the FBI launched 'Operation Final Answer' to gather the evidence they needed to catch the criminals and end the scam.

Twenty-five agents set to work, screening 20,000 telephone calls, which filled nearly 250 cassette tapes (ask a grown-up what they were). They later said it was one of the

most exciting cases they had ever worked on. The first breakthrough came when they discovered many of the big winners were not residents where they said they were but actually lived around Lawrenceville where Uncle Jerry was still living – by now luxuriously in a lakeside house surrounded by his valuable collection of vintage cars.

The net began to close. The FBI got McDonald's to help them with the operation, making a fake TV ad to flush out some of the fake winners by launching a new Monopoly

game to attract more fraudsters and build a stronger case against them. The plan worked and the evidence began to mount up that Uncle J and his pals were not lucky game players but HORRIBLE HEINOUS HEISTERS.

In 2001 Uncle Jerry and seven others were finally arrested (funnily enough, one of them actually came from a town called Fair Play). Uncle Jerry was questioned, and **confessed** that over the past twelve years or so he had taken **sixty of the winning tokens** for prizes worth a whopping total of **$24m**. In the end, fifty people were convicted, and some of them paid a heavy price. Uncle Jerry went to prison for three years and had to pay $12.5m of his takings back. No more classic cars for him. His nephew served one year in prison, and Mr Fisher (remember him from Jacksonville?) got three years' probation and had to pay back $300,000. Others were treated a bit more kindly, like Gloria, the single mum who found the prospect of a life-changing payday irresistible and was hoodwinked into a scheme that was murkier than she could ever have imagined. She was convicted but spared jail and ordered to pay back the money little by little. She now works two jobs to make ends meet.

And what of Uncle Jerry? After he served his time in jail, he returned to Florida, where he now leads a much quieter life. He is in poor health but is still in touch with some of his fellow fraudsters. Perhaps they meet up sometimes for a burger to reminisce?

And what of the innocent McDonald's customers who had bought a burger or milkshake hoping to win some prizes? Well, when the scam was exposed lots of them were furious that they had bought a ton of burgers to participate in a game they had no hope of winning. So McDonald's responded by launching an **Instant Cash Giveaway, handing out $10m to fifty-five random customers**, including a man who had been homeless and sleeping in a cardboard box. Some people thought that was not generous enough, so in one weekend McDonald's made millionaires of fifteen customers who just happened to go into participating restaurants that day.

McDonald's still runs the Monopoly game today and there are *still* tremendous prizes to be won, but they won't just come to you, you have to remember to actually go to McDonald's to claim them. That's right . . . lots of prizes *are* **unclaimed**, for example, fourteen Mini Cooper cars! So if *you* ever find any old McDonald's packaging that you carelessly stuffed down the back of your sofa, remember to check it carefully. Because with any luck, you might just end up driving away in a $30,000 car. Though PLEASE make sure you have a driving licence first.

THE END

Sources

The Tall Tale of the Eiffel Tower
'The Man Who Sold The Eiffel Tower. Twice.' *Smithsonian Magazine*. 9th March 2016.
https://www.smithsonianmag.com/history/man-who-sold-eiffel-tower-twice-180958370/

Has Anybody Seen My Brain?
'The Tragic Story Of How Einsteins Brain Was Stolen And Wasn't Even Special.' *National Geographic*. 21st April 2014.
https://www.nationalgeographic.com/premium/article/the-tragic-story-of-how-einsteins-brain-was-stolen-and-wasnt-even-special

The Lady Who Vanished
'The Curious Story Of The Man Who Stole The Mona Lisa.' Guinness World Records. 9th May 2023.
https://www.guinnessworldrecords.com/news/2023/5/the-curious-story-of-the-man-who-stole-the-mona-lisa-749918

A Gruesome, Grisly Gunpowder Plot
'What Is The Story Behind Bonfire Night?' Royal Museums Greenwich.
https://www.rmg.co.uk/stories/topics/gunpowder-plot-what-history-behind-bonfire-night

The Maple Syrup Mystery
'Canada's 'maple syrup heist' thief must repay millions for sweet stolen good'. The *Guardian*. 1st April 2022.
https://www.theguardian.com/world/2022/apr/01/maple-syrup-heist-theif-ordered-repay-stolen-goods-canada

The Millennium Dome Diamond Heist
'How The Police Beat The Dome Diamond Gang.' The *Guardian*. 7th November 2000. https://www.theguardian.com/uk/2000/nov/07/dome1

A Perfectly Preposterous Princess Prank
'The Mysterious Princess Caraboo.' The History Press. 2nd April 2017.
https://thehistorypress.co.uk/article/the-mysterious-princess-caraboo/

The Very Hungry Bear Break-in
'Hank The Tank, A 400-Pound Bear Behind Lake Tahoe Break-Ins, Is Captured.' *The New York Times*. 6th April 2023.
https://www.nytimes.com/2023/08/06/us/lake-tahoe-bear-hank-the-tank.html
https://www.independent.co.uk/news/world/americas/hank-tank-bear-california-homes-b2022821.html

The Fake Fairies of Cottingley
'Cottingley Fairies: How Sherlock Holmes's Creator Was Fooled By Hoax.' BBC News. 5th December 2020.
https://www.bbc.co.uk/news/uk-england-leeds-55187973

The Burglar and the Bugle
'French Waiter Admits Art Theft.' The *Guardian*. 23rd May 2022.
https://www.theguardian.com/world/2002/may/23/arttheft.arts

A Deadly Dangerous Bug Caper
'It's Tiger King Meets Ace Ventura': The Wild True Story Of The World's Biggest Insect Heist.' The *Guardian*. 23rd February 2022.
https://www.theguardian.com/tv-and-radio/2022/feb/23/bug-out-its-tiger-king-meets-ace-ventura-the-wild-true-story-of-the-worlds-biggest-insect-heist

The Million Dollar McDonald's Heist
'McMillions: The Stranger-Than-Fiction Story Of The $24-Million McDonald's Monopoly Theft.' *Vanity Fair*. 4th February 2020.
https://www.vanityfair.com/hollywood/2020/02/mcmillions-hbo-true-story?srsltid=AfmBOoreG1ZYiC61WnmCs0hyRZ81eZfpzbrTN1OzZuW4YTzKphi_8F9_

Acknowledgments

I would like to thank Emily Lunn,
Helen Archer and all at Wren & Rook.
Also thanks to my agent
Tim Bates and all at PFD.